A STONE'S THROW
FROM BETHLEHEM

To Dale

David Teeter

A STONE'S THROW FROM BETHLEHEM

CHRISTIANS, MUSLIMS, AND JEWS IN THE LAND OF PROMISE

DAVID TEETER

Outskirts Press, Inc.
Denver, Colorado

Contents

Part 2 – Footsteps of Christ in Islam

Part 3 – Sharing the Land of Promise

Acknowledgements

A Stone's Throw from Bethlehem is dedicated to the people of our Friendship Center in Bethlehem. Friendship Center was my wife Willow's idea. She found the way into the hearts of our Muslim friends. Our other long-term Bethlehem partners were:

Fred Mollon
Ivy (Mollon) Gauvin, and their children, Sarah and
    Christian
Duane Rogers

They worked long and hard in a challenging and sometimes dangerous situation to share Christ's love for Muslim people. It was their people skills and faithful service to Christ that made the difference.

Our short-term guest workers and student interns were also of great help. Our daughter Deborah came to help us several times when we most needed her, and is helping me with this book.

Project Redemption, our non-profit support organization, handed our logistics at home. Our home team included Diane Robinson, Carole McSwain, Howard Adao, and our daughters Karen, Tristie, and Deborah. They processed our finances and our newsletters, advocated for our ministry, and scheduled our furlough speaking tours.

We are deeply grateful to all of our supporting churches and individuals. Thanks also to World Vision International, whose grants helped fund our Friendship Center and Bethlehem Bible College.

Special thanks to our two proofreaders, Sandy Price and Deborah Teeter. Sandy also proofed my previous book, *The Days of the Prophets*.

We fondly remember Marie Hollowell, who first made us aware of the Palestinian people. She died in 2002. You will meet her in the Introduction to this book.

Preface

When we left Israel in 1989, I intended to write two books about our experiences. One book would be about our eleven years in Jerusalem and Bethlehem working with Christians, Muslims, and Jews. A second book would be about biblical prophecy.

However, I soon discovered that I was not ready to write either of these books. I made several starts, but each time I ran into an impenetrable "writer's block."

We had just lived through some of the most exciting and meaningful experiences of our lives. We had also barely survived a situation of extreme stress, heartbreak and moments of terror. Writing either book would have meant reliving these experiences. I could not do it.

Finally, after 19 years, the writing block has dissolved.

Resumed contacts with some of our Muslim friends helped provide the closure I needed.

I wrote my biblical prophecy book first, *The Days of the Prophets*, which was published in April of 2009. The day after it was published, I started writing *A Stone's Throw from Bethlehem–Christians, Muslims, and Jews in the Land of Promise.*

I still follow events in Israel and Palestine very carefully through contact with reliable Israeli and Palestinian sources. I also have my journals, research papers, and newsletters from our time in Israel. All of these sources have gone into *A Stone's Throw from Bethlehem*.

Some readers may complain that my account is biased. Of course it is. There is no such thing as an unbiased account of the Israeli-Palestinian conflict.

Even in Israel, there are many conflicting points of view of the conflict. Israeli "new historians" differ from the official Israeli government version. Jewish peace and human rights activists have one view; the settler movement has another.

Palestinian Christians have a very different view perspective than that of Christian Zionists.

My perspective is pro-Palestine, pro-Israel, and pro-peace. It reflects my years working with Israelis and Palestinians, Christians, Muslims, and Jews, as well as my background as a Bible scholar and teacher.

I support Israel's right to exist and live in peace with their Arab neighbors, including the Palestinians. I do not support policies that deny the same blessings of freedom to the Palestinian people. I strongly condemn all acts of violence by either side against the other's civilian population.

Books by David Teeter include:
- *The Kingdom Suffers Violence*, People's Bible Press, 1974. (Out of print, but used copies are sometimes available on Amazon.com).
- *The Days of the Prophets—What We Can Learn From Biblical Prophecy*, Outskirts Press, 2009
- *A Stone's Throw from Bethlehem—Christians, Muslims, and Jews in the Land of Promise*, Outskirts Press, 2009

For more information, visit my web site,
http://davidteeter.org.

Introduction

This is the story of our eleven years in Jerusalem and Bethlehem, living and working with Christians, Muslims, and Jews.

I have always had a love for Israel. I was thrilled when Israel became a state in 1948. My pastor told me, "Keep your eyes on Israel; Israel is God's prophecy signpost." I was twelve years old at the time.

As a young adult, I hardly knew that the Palestinian people existed. I only knew that Arabs were Israel's enemy, and God was on Israel's side.

A woman named Marie Hollowell first made us aware of the Palestinian people, and another side of the story.

Marie was the Dean of Women at Seattle Pacific College, where I met my wife Willow in 1954. It was Marie's job as Willow's housemother to run me out of the woman's dorm every evening at curfew time. We became dear friends.

Later, Marie went to Lebanon, where she worked at the Beirut College for Women. We would get together whenever she came to Seattle on furlough. I gave her my "pro-Israel" views, and she would tell me, "David, there is another side to the story." She told me of a trip she made to Bethlehem, and the people she met there. Her favorite saying was, "I just love them all."

This was the beginning of our journey to Jerusalem and Bethlehem. We too would learn to "love them all." This includes Palestinians as well as Israelis, whether they are Jews, Muslims, or Christians.

Our experiences in Jerusalem and Bethlehem brought us face to face with some difficult questions:

- Can we be both "pro-Israel" and "pro-Palestine?" How can we love our enemies, as Jesus commanded? Especially when our enemies mean us harm?
- Is it possible for a Muslim to follow Jesus without converting to the Christian religion? What does it mean to be a Muslim? What do Muslims know of Jesus?
- Is there any hope for peace between Israel and Palestine? What does scripture say about sharing the land of promise?

You will explore these questions as you read A *Stone's*

Throw from Bethlehem. There are three parts to this book:

- Part 1, *The Road to Bethlehem*, is the story of our interfaith work with Christians, Muslims, and Jews in Jerusalem and Bethlehem. It begins with Egyptian President Sadat's historic visit to Jerusalem in 1977. It concludes with our team caught in the middle of the Palestinian uprising (Intifada).

- Part 2, *Footsteps of Christ in Islam*, explores the concept of Muslim followers of Jesus. I discuss the essence of Islam, what Muslims know of Jesus, the difficult issues, and what this means for the gospel in the Muslim world.

- Part 3, *"Sharing the Land of Promise"*, explains why peace has been so elusive. I make a biblical case for Israelis and Palestinians sharing one homeland. You will learn the basis for my hopes for peace in the Middle East.

Part 1:
On the Road to Bethlehem

Leave your country, your people, and your father's household and go to the land I will show to you. (Gen. 12:1)

Lead us on the straight path, the path of those upon whom you have bestowed your grace. (Quran 1: 5, 6)

Whoever serves me must follow me; and where I am, my servant also will be. (John 12:26)

Ben Yehuda Street in West Jerusalem

CHAPTER 1

The Road to Jerusalem

My wife Willow knew something was up when she walked into our bedroom. I had posted a large map of East Africa and the Middle East on our bedroom wall.

She was right. We were about to embark on a long postponed adventure. Willow told me when we first started dating in college that she wanted to be a missionary. We both majored in cultural anthropology.

But life got in the way. We married in 1955. Our three daughters were born. The years went by.

It was now 1977. I had pastored my first two churches. I was now Director of People's Bible Institute and an Associate Pastor of People's Church in Tacoma, Washington.

Willow was teaching in the public schools. Our lives were full, but we both felt something was missing. With our children now grown, we both felt it was time to take another step in our journey of faith.

The map on the wall was my signal to Willow that her long postponed missionary calling was about to be realized.

We began exploring possibilities in East Africa and the Middle East. I have always had an interest in the Middle East. I had already led two tours to Israel, Egypt, Jordan, and Lebanon, in 1973 and 1976.

I contacted a friend, Costa Deir of Elim Fellowship, who often led seminars for local pastors in East Africa and the Middle East. Costa was born in Palestine to Greek Orthodox parents. He and his team were about to set out on a seminar tour to Egypt, Jordan, and Israel. He invited me to join the team, and I accepted.

In each country, I prayed and asked the Lord if this was where we should begin our Middle East work. The answer I seemed to get at each place was "not here, keep going."

"You choose": I did not get an answer to my prayers until after we completed our last seminar, in Jerusalem. Some of the Palestinian pastors told me of a need for a Christian college for the Arab Evangelical churches.

The rest of the team had returned home, but I stayed behind in Jerusalem to pray. One night while I was praying I told the Lord, "I only want to do your will. Do you want us to go to the Middle East? Or should we stay in Tacoma?"

The answer I got was, "You choose."

After some considerable inner debate, I finally told the Lord, "Ok, if I have to choose, we will begin our work in Jerusalem."

Confirmation came the next day. The news broke that Egyptian President Anwar Sadat was coming to Jerusalem to address the Israeli Knesset (Parliament).

President Sadat delivered his historic speech on November 20, 1977. His speech electrified the Israeli public and set the stage for Camp David and peace between Israel and Egypt.

That speech also started us on our road to Jerusalem and Bethlehem. It was our confirmation that a door of ministry was opening for us in the Holy Land.

Meanwhile, back in Tacoma, Willow had a powerful dream. In the dream, she saw herself working with Palestinian people in Jerusalem. We made the decision to proceed with preparations for ministry in Jerusalem and Bethlehem.

Elim Fellowship accepted us for sponsorship. Elim was the mission society which had sponsored our 1977 seminars in Egypt, Jordan, and Israel.

Once again, Costa Deir invited us to join his seminar team. This time our seminars would take us to the Congo, Tanzania, Burundi, Egypt, Jordan, and Israel. Our plan was to remain in Jerusalem at the end of the tour.

Saying goodbye: I resigned from my post as director of People's Bible Institute in Tacoma; Willow resigned her public school teaching position. We spent the summer of 1978 speaking in churches to raise our support. Our own church made a substantial support commitment.

Our oldest daughter Karen was married in June. Tristie, our second daughter, married on September 1. I officiated at both weddings. Our youngest daughter Debbie graduated from high school. The University of Washington accepted her as a student. Deborah would stay with family friends while studying at the UW.

We sold our home in Tacoma, kissed our daughters goodbye, and boarded the flight to New York to meet up with the other team members at Elim. I spent my forty-second birthday in the air on a long flight to Kinshasa, Zaire (now the Congo).

In Africa, Willow discovered she was seriously allergic to mangos. She broke out with a rash and was very sick. She claims I took her to the local witch doctor, but not so. I took her to a nice, French trained woman doctor. She gave Willow a shot that helped with the symptoms, and we continued on to Tanzania, Burundi, Egypt, and Jordan.

We arrived in Jerusalem on November 11, 1978, almost a year after Sadat's historic visit to Israel.

It was bitterly cold, windy, and rainy. We had been traveling for four weeks in tropical Africa and were not dressed for Jerusalem weather. We almost froze until a shipment arrived from home with our winter clothing.

Our initial vision: We started out in Jerusalem with three objectives:

1. Strengthen the Christian Arab community. We would explore the feasibility of establishing a Bible College for the evangelical churches in the land.

2. Do field research toward a doctorate at Fuller Seminar. Willow would do research for a master's degree.

3. Find some way to connect our faith in Christ with Muslim people. We did not yet have a clear idea of how this would happen.

First, we had to find a place to live and learn how to cope with the language, culture, and oddities of two conflicting societies.

CHAPTER 2

Jerusalem West and East

Jerusalem is a unique city. It is the "holy city" of Judaism, Islam, and Christianity. West Jerusalem is a Jewish city. East Jerusalem is an Arab city. The "Old City" inside its high walls is divided into Muslim, Jewish, Christian, and Armenian Quarters.

When we first arrived in Jerusalem, we stayed for several weeks in a guest apartment in an Arab neighborhood in East Jerusalem.

We then found an apartment in West Jerusalem, which we leased for one year. This apartment was in a Jewish neighborhood called "Ramat Eschol."

WEST JERUSALEM

Secular versus Ultra-Orthodox: The divisions between secular and ultra-Orthodox Jews are almost as bitter as between Jews and Arabs. In fact, some ultra-

Orthodox sects even opposed the creation of the State of Israel.

Ramat Eschol was a secular Jewish neighborhood. A block away was an ultra-Orthodox neighborhood called "Sanhedria." It got its name from the tombs scattered in little parks throughout the neighborhood. These may be tombs of the members of the Sanhedrin, the high court of the Jewish people in Jesus' time.

On Friday evenings, we heard the noisy clashes between the ultra-Orthodox and secular Jews. Jewish settlers would drive into Jerusalem on Shabbat (the Sabbath). The road took them past Sanhedria. The Haridim (ultra-Orthodox) would stand at the top of the hill and throw stones at the settlers passing below.

The police would charge the hill and push the Haridim out of stone throwing range. Of course, no one intentionally drove **into** any of the Ultra-Orthodox neighborhoods on Shabbat, for they would certainly be stoned. The police barricaded those streets every Shabbat evening to prevent incidents.

Our Jewish neighbors: I remember walking to our neighborhood grocery store for the first time. I saw a loaf of bread lying on the sidewalk outside of the store. As I watched, a bomb squad van pulled up beside the sinister bread. A heavily armored police sapper (bomb specialist) picked up the loaf of bread, placed it in a steel container in the back of the van, and left.

I told Willow when I got home that I had seen a loaf of bread get arrested. We soon learned that any unattended package gets this same treatment, and for good reason.

A few months later, someone put a bomb inside a flower pot. It exploded inside of the grocery store injuring the security guard.

One of the buses we often took to downtown Jerusalem was also bombed. Fortunately, we were not on board at the time.

It took us a while to get acclimated to life in Israel. Of course, the language barrier was the biggest problem. Shopping was a problem at first. Many familiar products were not available, or were packaged in some way we didn't recognize.

We did not have a car so we took the bus everywhere. Israelis do not like to stand in line. At the bus stop, a crowd forms and everyone tries to get on the bus at the same time. There is an Israeli saying: "The line at the bank forms one deep—and ten wide." I learned to set aside my polite upbringing, and push and shove with everyone else.

Our Orthodox neighbor upstairs: While we were away on a trip, an Orthodox couple, Devorah and Yossi, moved into the apartment directly above us. Our secular Jewish neighbors were appalled, fearing that this was the beginning of an Orthodox takeover of our neighborhood.

On Shabbat (Sabbath), the Orthodox couple yelled at the neighbors to turn off their radios and televisions.

Orthodox Jews are not supposed to use electrical switches during Shabbat. When expecting guests on Shabbat, they would prop open the outside door with a stone.

Our secular neighbors retaliated by removing the stone, letting the door close and lock. Our Orthodox neighbor's guests would have to yell for someone to let them in. Willow or I would go down and let the guests into the building.

Willow decided to make friends with Devorah and Yossi. She went up and knocked on their door. When Devorah came to the door, Willow invited her to tea or coffee in our apartment. Willow knew that Deborah, being Orthodox, would have to decline coming to our apartment, since we did not maintain a kosher kitchen.

When Devorah declined, Willow said, "OK, then I'll have coffee with you in your apartment." Devorah invited her in, and that was the beginning of a good friendship.

Sukkot (Feast of Tabernacles) is a fall festival. Jews build booths outside their homes and eat their meals there during the seven days of Sukkot.

Yossi was having trouble with his Sukkah (booth). It kept falling down. He struggled with it until sundown, when he had to stop for Shabbat. I was away on a trip, so Willow finished putting up Yossi's Sukkah. She also carried his toolbox upstairs for him, since he could not carry it on Shabbat.

When we moved out of our apartment, Devorah cried. She told Willow we were her only friends in the building.

Dr. Lev's Jewish-Arab youth club: We met a Jewish man, Dr. Lev Yakir-Am, who founded a Jewish-Arab youth club called "Meditran." Dr. Yakir-Am had once served as the science advisor to the Prime Minister.

The club offered classes in Hebrew for Arab youths and in Arabic for Jewish youths. Willow volunteered to teach English to both. The club provided other social and recreational activities as well. I taught and played chess.

BAPTIST HOUSE

On Saturdays, we worshipped with the Narkis Street Baptist Congregation. This church was located in a Jewish neighborhood several blocks from downtown West Jerusalem. We called the church and its bookstore "Baptist House." A friendly Reform Jewish congregation was our church's nearest neighbor.

Baptist House had a multi-national congregation. Many were foreign students at Hebrew University. Others were working for Israeli or Christian service agencies. Most were Israeli-oriented. A few, like us, were working on the Arab side. Messianic Jews and Christian Arabs worshipped side by side.

Dr. Robert (Bob) Lindsay was the pastor of the church. He had lived in Israel for more than forty years.

Bob Lindsay was a colorful and charismatic figure, known and admired by Israelis and Palestinians alike.

He had a wooden leg, which he sometimes took off and waved around to make a point. He had lost that leg to a land mine while rescuing a Palestinian child trapped in "no man's land." (This was before the 1967 war.)

Bob was a noted Hebrew and Greek scholar. He and his wife Margaret became two of our dearest friends in Israel. Bob invited me to serve on his pastoral council, which we called the "Ro'im" (shepherds). The Ro'im served as a board of elders, a rather unusual arrangement for a Baptist Church. I also served several terms as Moderator of the congregation.

Services were on Saturday because Sunday is a normal workday in Israel. This left me free to visit Christian Arab churches on Sundays.

The Church Firebombed: The night of October 7, 1982, our Narkis Street Baptist church was firebombed and destroyed by arsonists. According to the police, the arsonists were members of a Jewish extremist group called "Kach" (Thus!).

But that was not the end of "Baptist House." We got permission from Mayor Teddy Kollek to put up a tent on site as a temporary place of worship. We applied for a permit to rebuild. The Mayor and city council approved our request. But the planning commission rejected our application. We appealed all the way to Israel's High (Supreme)

Court. We won the appeal, but it still took eight years and a second trip to the High Court to get our permit.

Meanwhile, our "temporary" tent grew larger and more solid. We built a wooden floor for the tent. We replaced the canvas sides with corrugated aluminum panels. Then we built a plywood roof to support the canvas top.

Our "tent" was big enough to hold the 300 people who regularly attended our Saturday services. In Israel, there is nothing quite as permanent as a temporary arrangement!

President Carter's visit: Bob Lindsay and I took a business trip to Cyprus. We shared a hotel room in Nicosia.

While in Cyprus, Bob received a phone call from his wife Margaret. President Carter was coming to Jerusalem to address the Israeli Knesset. President and Mrs. Carter would be attending church on Sunday, and Bob, as the ranking Baptist in Israel, was to preach the sermon. We cut our Cyprus meetings short and flew back to Israel.

Our "Baptist House" church was checked out for security. It failed the test. So President Carter's service was moved to Saint Andrew's Church, which was better situated for security purposes. Bob preached the sermon. Willow and I attended as part of the Baptist delegation. The Carters sat in the pew just behind us.

President Carter looked very tired. He had flown from Egypt the night before, and had been up past midnight talking to Prime Minister Begin. He shook hands with us after the service and then left immediately for talks with the Israeli cabinet.

Jimmy Carter's deep devotion made a strong impression on me. I am glad he found the spiritual resources he needed for his negotiations with Egypt and Israel.

EAST JERUSALEM

East Jerusalem is the Arab side of Jerusalem. However, the municipality of Jerusalem has been pushing into East Jerusalem and the Old City. Jewish establishments are taking over many of the buildings and building sites.

Sundays, we usually worshipped in the Arab Baptist Church in East Jerusalem. I often preached the sermon.

During the week, we visited Christian Arab members in their homes. We took several trips to Ramallah in the West Bank and to the Galilee to preach in Christian Arab churches there.

We were learning to live in two worlds simultaneously—Jewish and Arab. The two cultures are very different. Israeli Jews tend to be very brusque and outspoken. Arabs have elaborate polite social rituals and sayings for every occasion.

But everyone was very patient with us while we learned.

Our Research Project: Before leaving for Israel, Fuller Seminary had accepted me into a doctoral program.

My plan was to do two years of outside research and study in Israel, and then return to Fuller for additional course work and to write my dissertation.

In Jerusalem, Dr. Joseph Haddad, Director of Studies at St. George's College, agreed to supervise my doctoral research on behalf of Fuller Seminary. My plan was to study relationships between Christian and Muslim communities in the land.

Dr. Haddad introduced me to a notable Muslim authority, Dr. Haazam Khalidi. Sheikh Khalidi tutored me in the Islamic religion.

Willow was also starting her research for a Master's thesis in anthropology.

As part of this research, we began visiting the homes of Christian Arabs, and getting their perspectives on Christian-Muslim relationships.

We had yet to find a way to connect with the Muslim community, although we had studied Arab culture as part of our anthropology majors.

Rural Christian Villages: We finally were able to buy a car. My study program qualified me with Israeli customs to buy a car with a reduced customs duty (25% instead of 100%). We bought a little blue Ford Fiesta. Made in Spain, it had a tiny 900 cc engine, (probably meant for a sewing machine.) Nevertheless, it was low geared, and quite able to grind its way up the many hills. It served us well for our remaining ten years in Israel and Palestine.

Now we were able to get out into the countryside and visit some of the Christian Palestinian villages. Christian villages in the West Bank are clustered around Ramallah and Bethlehem. Ramallah is about 15 miles north of Jerusalem, and Bethlehem is 7 miles south of Jerusalem.

One such village was **Taibeh**. This village is on the edge of the desert about five miles northeast of Ramallah. From this village there is a steep road with many switchbacks down to Jericho. Joshua and his army climbed up this route to attack the town of Ai. We preferred to drive down this road, rather than up it. (Josh. 8)

Village tradition holds that Taibeh is the village of Ephraim, where Jesus hid out for a time after the raising of Lazarus. (John 11:54)

In the village, there are ruins of an ancient church built to commemorate Jesus' stay in the village. Christians gather there on Sunday evenings to light oil lamps and pray.

We were surprised to learn that local Christian families sometimes sacrifice a sheep in front of the church when they have a special need or want to give thanks for some blessing or healing. The blood is dabbed on the sides of the doorframe, much as we read in the Exodus story. We could see the blood stains from recent sacrifices. The people do not burn the sheep on an altar. Instead, they eat the sheep, a much better idea.

Sirhan Sirhan, Bobby Kennedy's assassin, was born in this village. His family still lives there.

We also visited the Galilean village of **Kfar Yasif**. This village is about 7 miles northwest of Nazareth. It was once the home of the Jewish historian Josephus. (His Jewish name was Joseph Ben Matthias.) It is now a mixed Christian and Muslim village. I preached in an evangelical and an Anglican Church in Kfar Yasif.

Easter terror: On one Easter morning, armed men from a neighboring Druze village attacked the town of Kfar Yasif. The Druze attackers destroyed many houses, cars, and businesses. The only fatalities were two Kfar Yasif policemen.

This attack was revenge for a Druze youth killed in a soccer riot. During the game the Druze fans got upset with the referee's decisions. They started throwing grenades at the referees. The Kfar Yasif fans regarded this as poor sportsmanship. The fans started fighting and a Druze youth was stabbed. He died later in the hospital

The Druze people have their own religion. They look back to the Midianite Jethro, Moses' father-in-law, as their prophet. They serve in the Israeli army and border police and are heavily armed with jeeps, machine guns, and anti-tank rockets, all of which they used against Kfar Yasif.

Thankfully, the members of the churches where we preached were not injured.

We were keeping busy with our Christian Arab churches. However, we had not yet found a way to connect with the Muslim people of the land.

Our blue license plate: An earlier attempt did not work out as well. It happened the day we took delivery of our shiny blue Ford Fiesta. We decided to take a drive out into the West Bank to a Muslim village several miles north of Jerusalem.

As we drove into the village, we saw the hostile looks of the children and youth. When we turned around to drive out, we saw that children had put a barricade of stones across the road. Some of the youths were standing by with rocks in their hands. They did not look at all friendly or inviting.

Fortunately, we were able to navigate through the blockade and left with our shiny new Fiesta intact.

We later learned why we received this hostile response. Our car had yellow Israeli license plates. Arab West Bank cars have blue license plates. The children, seeing our yellow plates, assumed we were Jewish settlers scouting out their village.

They had good reason to be worried. Several years later, a Jewish settlement confiscated their farm lands and the villagers had to move.

For the next ten years, our yellow license plate proved both a blessing and a hindrance. It eased our way through Israeli checkpoints, but we were sometimes mistaken for Jewish settlers. We were at risk of getting stoned.

On one occasion, Willow coerced one of our Christian Arab friends to drive us out into the countryside southeast of Bethlehem. We drove into a remote village called "Seir."

There was a well in the center of the village. Women were filling water pots at the well and carrying them home on their heads, just like pictures of ancient times.

Willow wanted to get out of the car and talk to the women at the well, but our driver was afraid. So we drove on. Willow determined that one day she would go back and talk to those women at the well. This she did, but that will be a later story.

Willow still wanted to get out into the Muslim villages, so she volunteered to work with an international health team that operated clinics in rural villages. She was able to visit several rural Muslim villages in the West Bank. But most of the villages remained inaccessible to us.

BETHLEHEM BIBLE COLLEGE

A number of Christian Palestinian educators and pastors had formed a committee to start a Bible college. They had seen that their youth who left for college abroad seldom returned to help their own people.

In Israel and the Palestinian territories, religion is a required subject. Students must pass an exam in their own religion to graduate from high school. Schools in villages or towns with a Christian Arab population are required to teach the Christian religion. The same applies to schools with Muslim or Jewish students. And this applies even to the government schools.

Bethlehem Bible College was set up initially to train

Christian Arabs to teach the Christian religion in schools with Christian students, both in Israel and in the Palestinian territories.

I was familiar with academic accrediting standards for Bible Colleges in the USA. The committee asked me to design an academic program for the College. I became the founding academic dean of the College.

This was the beginning of Bethlehem Bible College. Dr. Bishara Awad was and is the founding president. Bishara was born in Jerusalem. A stray bullet killed his father during the 1948 war.

Bishara was educated in an orphanage school, and later went to college in the USA. After teaching for some years in the USA, he returned to become the headmaster of the Hope Secondary School in the village of Beit Jala near Bethlehem.

Later, Willow took Bishara to meet Dr. Lev and visit the Jewish-Arab youth club. We were all shocked to learn the clubhouse was once the Awad family home, where Bishara's father was shot and killed during the 1948 war.

Classes began at the Bible College in the fall of 1979. We held our first classes in the Lutheran Church in Bethlehem. We later moved classes to the Hope Secondary School in Beit Jala. Still later, the college was able to lease the top floor of a new municipal building in Bethlehem.

Bethlehem is in the occupied West Bank territory. Palestinians in the territories do not have the protection of Israeli law. At that time, Israeli army administrators handled most Palestinian civil matters. This included the licensing of Palestinian colleges and universities.

Bethlehem Bible College received its license from the Israeli military and began classes in 1979. We graduated our first class in June of 1981.

The college has since expanded into an accredited four-year college. It offers a number of community programs in addition to its biblical curriculum. It has branches in Nazareth and Gaza City (although the Gaza branch is presently closed due to the military closure of Gaza).

This completed our first year in Israel. We had made many Jewish friends. We had preached in many of the Christian Arab churches in Jerusalem, the Galilee, and the West Bank territories. We had helped start a Palestinian Bible College.

Now it was time to leave our apartment in West Jerusalem and move out into the occupied West Bank territory. Our next home would be in the village of Beit Jala, on the outskirts of Bethlehem.

CHAPTER 3

Bethlehem and Vicinity

Bethlehem is not in Israel proper. It is located in the West Bank territory captured from Jordan in the 1966 war. Bethlehem is six miles south of Jerusalem. Leaving Jerusalem meant leaving Israel and moving to occupied Palestine.

Bethlehem is the largest of three traditionally Christian towns located six miles south of Jerusalem. Beit Jala was built on a steep hill to the west of Bethlehem. Locals called this hill "Mt. Everest."

Beit Sahur is the third Christian Arab village. It is a smaller village about a mile east and down the hill from Bethlehem. The traditional "shepherd's fields" where angels appeared are on the outskirts of Beit Sahur.

BEIT JALA.

Before 1948, the population of Beit Jala was 100%

Christian. When we lived there, its population included 6,000 Christian Arabs and 2,000 Muslims. Many of the Christians had fled during the 1948 and 1967 wars. We were told that 40,000 former Beit Jala residents now live in Lima, Peru.

Bethlehem and Beit Jala were settled in Islamic times by two different Christian Arab tribes. During the wars of the 7th century, one tribe allied itself to the Byzantines. The other tribe became allies of the Persians.

The enmity from this period has persisted into modern times. Beit Jala women wore a red veil, and Bethlehem women wore a white veil as tribal symbols. It was considered shameful for a Bethlehem girl to marry a Beit Jala man or visa-versa.

Our Christian Arab informants told us that a notorious witch lived in Beit Jala. There were stories of village men folk being enticed by promises of gold to go into a cave and were never seen again. We were a little surprised at the legends of witchcraft and magic believed by these devout evangelical believers. We met the witch once, but never saw the cave (or the gold).

Our new home was a basement apartment in a small two-story house. Three elderly sisters owned the house and lived upstairs. The walls were of two-foot thick stone. The house had a lovely garden in the back with olive and other fruit trees.

The house was located in the valley, just a stone's throw from Bethlehem. Manger Square, with its Church of the

Nativity, was about a 20-minute walk up the hill from our house.

Olga, the oldest sister had served in the Ministry of Education under King Hussein of Jordan in 1966. The three sisters watched and fussed over us. We loved them all.

There was a fourth sister. She was killed when Menachim Begin's Irgun group blew up the King David Hotel, in 1946. The explosion also trapped Lubbah, one of the remaining three sisters, in the rubble of the hotel, but she survived.

The three sisters used to own a large gracious home in a Jewish neighborhood in Jerusalem. They showed us the house where they once lived. Their father had been a well-liked university professor. He assumed that the family would be safe in their home when their neighborhood fell to the Israelis during the 1948 war.

However, Israeli fighters fired a machine gun through their window and ordered them to leave. They were not allowed to stop even to pack their family pictures. They left with just the clothes on their backs. Fortunately, they were able to move to this small house in Beit Jala.

So far, our ministry had been limited to the Christian Arab population. I continued to teach at the Bible College and preach occasionally in the Arab churches. However, our hearts ached to find some way to introduce Jesus to the Muslim community. Our big breakthrough came in the fall of 1980.

BETHLEHEM UNIVERSITY

Willow got a position teaching English at Bethlehem University. This is a Catholic university, run by the Christian Brothers order. The vast majority of students are Muslim. They come from towns, rural villages, and refugee camps throughout the West Bank and Gaza Strip.

The Catholic administration was worried about offending the majority Muslim community. They cautioned Willow and the other foreign teachers not to talk about religion or God in their classrooms.

Willow and her Muslim students: Willow does not like to "hide her light under a bushel." She wrote on her blackboard, "I believe in God."

She claimed she was just giving them an example of an English sentence, with noun, verb, preposition, and object.

Her Muslims students were not offended. In fact, they were amazed and intrigued that an educated American woman actually believed in God.

Aisha was one of Willow's Muslim women students. One day, Israeli soldiers surrounded the University and started shooting. Suddenly, all of Willow's students left the classroom except for Aisha.

Willow had no idea what was going on. She asked Aisha, "What are we supposed to do now?" Aisha answered, "We run, teacher." Willow asked, "Where do we go?" Aisha said, "Your house, teacher." That is how Aisha began coming to our house after school.

(**Note:** I have changed all the names of our Muslim student friends to protect their privacy.)

Kariim was another of Willow's Muslim students. He lived in a nearby refugee camp, and was a strict, devout Muslim. He brought us to his home in the refugee camp to meet his family. We came to love him as a son. After he graduated, we attended his wedding. He still speaks of Willow as a mother.

One of Kariim's friends came to Willow's class who had not registered with the University. Willow correctly refused to let him into her class. Kariim came to our home hoping to plead the cause of his friend.

To curry her favor, he bought us a clock mounted in a plastic moose head. It was not very Palestinian, or our taste in art, but we mounted it on our wall anyway. Willow tutored Kariim's friend off-campus until he was able to gain official admission to the college.

One day Willow got impatient and told her class: "You've made me so frustrated I'm going home and beat up my husband!" This they wanted to see. Four of her male students escorted Willow home to protect me from her wrath. When they saw how big I was, they realized I did not need their protection.

However, they were curious about how we lived. They started dropping in after class. It was not safe for them to travel alone, so each one brought a friend. That friend, in turn, would bring another friend. Soon we had a houseful of Muslim students almost every day.

One of the English classes Willow taught at the university was for High School English teachers. Some of the teachers had just been released from Israeli prisons.

Willow told them, "I know a song written by a man while in prison." The man was the apostle Paul. The song was *"Rejoice in the Lord always, and again I say rejoice."* (Phil. 4:4). We could sing it in both English and Arabic. She taught the English version to her English students.

Some five years later, a young Muslim student from the nearby refugee came to our Friendship Center. He sang for us, *"Rejoice in the Lord always, and again I say rejoice."* We asked him, "Where did you learn that song?" He said he had learned it from a friend in a rural village. He told us, "Oh, everyone knows this song. They sing it in all the schools around here."

Jesus spoke of the Kingdom of Heaven spreading like leaven in dough. We had a glimpse of how this could happen in Palestine.

A Christmas feast for Muslims: Our Muslim students are well aware of Christmas, because of all the tourist festivities in Bethlehem's Manger Square. But as Muslims, they were generally excluded.

Aisha was curious about how we celebrate Christmas in our own home. She asked to stay in our home over the Christmas break.

We told her she would need her father's permission. He was a very important Muslim religious leader in the community. He gave Aisha his permission.

Aisha said she wanted a Bible for Christmas. We bought her one. She read it from cover to cover by February. Her father read it also and it circulated through the family.

Kariim was also curious about Christmas. His impression of Christmas was based on what he had seen in Manger Square—foreign tourists getting drunk and making out on Christmas Eve.

We saw Christmas as an opening for sharing our joy in Christ with our Muslim friends. We knew that the story of Jesus' birth is in the Quran. We determined to hold a special Christmas feast for all our Muslim friends.

No Arab celebration is complete without a feast, and that is not just tea and cookies! That first Christmas we served at least sixty dinners. We made mountains of rice, turkey, salads, and oranges—plus Christmas cookies which we baked by the gross. (Willow reminds me that she cut them all out by hand. Only in later years did someone send us Christmas pattern cookie cutters).

Because Muslims use a different calendar, they were not sure which day to come. So they came and came and came. Our Christmas feast stretched out to seven days.

We were exhausted by the time it ended. We flew to Cyprus for a week of R & R. This became our post-Christmas custom.

Our Christmas feast for Muslims became an annual

event. We did manage to cut it back to three days, and later, one or two days.

Students brought their families from villages and refugee camps throughout the West Bank and Gaza Strip. They all wanted to have their picture taken in front of our Christmas tree.

In turn, our students invited us to their homes in the rural villages and refugee camps. Willow became famous throughout the southern half of the West Bank for her hand puppets, she used to tell Bible stories to the women and small children.

The dark streets of Bethlehem: After our students went home, we would walk up the hill on Christmas Eve through the darkened streets to Manger Square in Bethlehem. Here and there, we would pass one or two Israeli soldiers on duty, huddling over a flickering oil lamp. There were soldiers also at the checkpoint at the entrance to Manger Square.

Walking through the dark streets at Christmas reminded us of what Bethlehem might have been like in Roman times, with Joseph, Mary, and the baby Jesus.

One year, Willow, and her teacher friend Jean, attended the midnight mass at the Church of the Nativity. They stayed around after the service and watched as cloistered nuns came out from neighboring convents for their own time of worship in the Church of the Nativity. For some of them, this was the only time they ventured out of their cells in their convent.

Our team grows: Our small apartment had evolved into an informal off-campus center for Muslim university students. We were now running ourselves ragged and we needed more help. Our youngest daughter Deborah came to help. She stayed with us off and on during our years in Bethlehem.

To solidify our support, I set up our own non-profit corporation, *Project Redemption*, based in Tacoma, Washington. I served as International Director.

We recruited one of my former Bible students in Tacoma, Duane Rogers. Duane spoke some Arabic, which was an immediate help, as I was still struggling with my Arabic lessons.

Next, Fred Mollon joined us as a student intern. After graduating from Elim, he returned with his wife Ivy and their two children, Christian (3) and Sarah (5).

The Mollon family arrived just as trouble broke out at Bethlehem University.

THE BABYLONIAN EXILE

Universities can become hotbeds of political protest. Bethlehem University was no exception. The Israeli army took a harsh response to all forms of student activism. It was a crime to display the Palestinian flag. Soldiers arrested Palestinian students even for wearing the colors of the Palestinian flag.

A high wall surrounds the University. Students would

barricade themselves in behind the walls, put up Palestinian flags, and hold demonstrations against the occupation.

Israeli soldiers would lob tear gas grenades over the walls. Israeli snipers would fire into the campus from neighboring rooftops. A bullet once missed Willow by inches as she was standing in the hallway outside her second-story classroom.

Once, Willow brought home an expended tear gas canister. She wanted me to see its "Made in the USA" trademark. Unfortunately, there was still some gas left in the canister. We had a houseful of guests from Jerusalem at the time. Our guests decided to leave when the gas started leaking into our crowded apartment. (In time, we learned to tolerate tear gas fairly well.)

In the fall of 1982, clashes between students and soldiers escalated. Closures became more frequent and lasted longer.

Willow and the other teachers were struggling to get in enough classes so the seniors could graduate. Willow and the other teachers began meeting off-campus with their students for homework assignments and exams.

In December, the military told the foreign teachers their work permits would not be renewed. They would have to leave the country at the end of the school year.

We decided this would be a time for us to take a long furlough. Fred and Ivy had established good rapport with our students, so we left them in charge of our informal "Friendship Center" for Muslim students.

I accepted a teaching and administrative position for the 1983-84 school year with the International Bible College in San Antonio, Texas.

But Willow was not ready to give up her dream of an off-campus "Friendship Center" for our Muslim friends. So before setting off for "darkest Texas," I applied for a grant from World Vision.

Darkest Texas: We spent the 1983-1984 school year teaching at IBC in San Antonio. Texas seemed more foreign to us than Israel or Palestine. Willow was also grieving for the students she had left behind in Bethlehem.

Shortly before Christmas, we received word that World Vision had approved our grant. During the Christmas break, Willow flew back to Israel and started looking for facilities for our Friendship Center.

She found an apartment building, which was still under construction. It was just down the road from our Beit Jala apartment. She negotiated a lease and put down a deposit for four apartments.

As soon as our school year ended in Texas, we drove back to Tacoma to see our daughters. Willow flew on back to Bethlehem ahead of me while I stayed behind to raise some more support. I returned to Bethlehem at summer's end.

We refer to our year in Texas as our "Babylonian exile." We were so glad to get back to Bethlehem.

CHAPTER 4

Return to Bethlehem

Back in Bethlehem, I resumed teaching at the Bible College. Willow did not return to Bethlehem University. Our new Friendship Center for Muslim students had become her full time job. The students were coming in droves.

OUR FRIENDSHIP CENTER IN BEIT JALA

The building Willow leased was in the valley one block below our previous apartment. It was in the middle of an olive grove at the end of a long lane. We were still in Beit Jala, but closer to the Aida refugee camp where Kariim lived.

The ground floor apartment became our Friendship Center. This apartment provided us with a social room, a kitchen, a recreation room for ping-pong, and an enclosed porch used as a study room. The other apartments provided living quarters for our team, including a guest apartment.

Our Center was open six days a week from 9 AM to 9 PM. Students dropped in before, between, and after classes. Most stayed several hours. About 150 different students came to our Center, averaging about 30 students per day.

The students who came to our Center were from the nearby towns, refugee camps, and rural villages in the West Bank and Gaza Strip.

The students were Sunni Muslims since this is the Islam of Palestine. Some were very devout and faithful in their Muslim observances. Others were more nominal in their observances. A few were rather indifferent about their faith. We also had a few Arab Christian students from the neighborhood.

Activities included conversation, table games, ping-pong, and TV. Students could do their homework in our study room. We kept some simple foods in the refrigerator, which they could fix for themselves if they were hungry.

We maintained a relaxed family atmosphere. We offered our love and friendship unconditionally. They responded. We were able to establish a relationship of mutual respect and trust.

We responded to their questions and asked plenty of our own. We discussed with them the Bible and the Quran. We pointed out common stories and shared religious values. We discussed our differences frankly, but with respect for each other's points of view.

We did not present formal religion classes in our Center. Instead, we learned from each other over many hours of informal discussion between playing chess, ping-pong, watching TV, and other center activities.

We did not try to convert our Muslim friends to Christianity, for reasons we will discuss in Part 2 of this book. We did want our Muslim friends to know Jesus as we knew him.

We told them, in essence, "We are all like sheep who have wandered away. God sent Jesus to bring us back. We are following Jesus. Jesus is not just for Christians. He is for Muslim people too. You are welcome to walk beside us and see what we can learn from each other."

The outcome of these conversations is the subject of Part 2, "Muslim Followers of Jesus."

The students kept coming even though Willow was no longer teaching at the university. Students were recruiting students.

CHRISTMAS IN OUR NEW FRIENDSHIP CENTER

Our first Christmas after our return from San Antonio marked a high point in our Bethlehem adventure.

We began on December 19 by setting up and decorating the Christmas tree. We invited our Muslim guys to help decorate the tree. Some of them brought ornaments. One brought a small plastic chick.

I also made some posters with stories of Jesus' birth from Matthew, Luke, and the Quran. The Quran has a beautiful story of Jesus' birth that parallels Luke but with an Arabian flavor.

The posters generated much discussion and criticism of my labored calligraphy. I did not take it personally because I knew that the students always criticized each other's calligraphy.

We served 137 dinners over a full seven-day feast. Three things happened that made this our memorable Christmas:

Mahmud and the Canadians: We were short of help, so Willow went up to the Bible College to seek out some volunteers. There she met two Canadian young men who had been backpacking through Europe and Israel. They had stopped at the Bible College hoping for a place to sleep.

They looked able-bodied and not weirder than the usual tourist youths. Willow grabbed them and dragged them down the hill to our Friendship Center. She put them to work baking cookies. They stayed with us for ten days and proved to be helpful and delightful guests.

Mahmud, one of our Muslim village friends wandered into the kitchen while they were making cookies. He looked the Canadians over carefully.

He told them: "I've learned from David and Willow that there are two kinds of Christians: Real Christians who believe in Jesus and are trying to follow Him. And there are those who are Christians in name only, and not real believers. Which kind are you?"

Mahmud's question stunned the two Canadians. Both were from evangelical backgrounds. One had made a previous commitment to Christ, but the other was still undecided. They had come to Bethlehem hoping for some answers to their doubts.

They were too embarrassed to admit to this Muslim youth that they did not know. They tried to evade the question.

But Mahmud was not going let them off the hook. He pressed them for two straight hours. Finally, the two Canadians called for me to get them out of the hot seat.

As a result, our Canadian guests made their commitment to Christ. They later wrote us from home about their renewed church activities.

Miracles still happen at Christmas. What greater miracle than two doubtful Christians rediscovering their faith in Christ with the help of a Muslim youth.

Jesus, the Light of the World: One night we turned on our Christmas tree lights. One of our Muslim guys, a Bedouin from the Gaza Strip exclaimed: "Jesus is the light of the world!" I said, "yes, but how did you know that?" He said, "From that book." He showed me a Bible he had been reading in our library.

A Candlelight Conversation: The next evening was Christmas Eve. After the students left, we turned off all but the Christmas tree lights and lit some candles for a quiet time of worship and reflection as a team.

A group of our Muslim students came back to the center after dinner, sat down, and quietly observed our devotions. After a while, they returned home to their student house. We wondered what they thought about our devotional time.

The next night, the same guys returned. One of them turned on the Christmas tree lights, another turned off the other lights, and another lit the candles. They asked, "Now, tell us everything you know about Jesus." That conversation went on until well after midnight.

SIX WEEKS IN BETHLEHEM

To augment our small team, we started a short-term guest worker program. Guests could live with us for six weeks. They would work in our Friendship Center for four weeks, with two weeks off for touring Israel.

This worked out really well. Most of our guest helpers were able to relate to the guys, and proved to be a real help. They were often invited to the homes of our Muslim guys to meet their families. It was so exciting no one wanted to take the full two weeks off to tour Israel. Most preferred to go on several day trips, spent a night or two in the Galilee, and return to the Center where the action was.

Most of our guest helpers came from the churches in America who supported us. They were of all ages. The enthusiasm they brought home with them was a great help in maintaining our support base.

We also started a longer-term student internship program. American college students stayed with us from three months to a year, earning college credit for working with our Muslim students in our Friendship Center.

There were very few problems with our guest workers and interns. Most did a wonderful job and were a real blessing to our Muslim friends and us. Only one or two of our "six week" guests failed to grasp the very sensitive position we were in between the Israeli military and the PLO. They did not feel it necessary to observe our ground rules on where to go and who to see. Regretfully, we could not allow them to stay.

DEALING WITH THE AUTHORITIES

We were between a "rock and a hard place" with the authorities. We had to have permission from the Israeli military to live and work in the occupied territories. At the same time, we needed at least the tacit permission of the Palestinian Liberation Organization (PLO) as well as the Muslim authorities to work with our Palestinian Muslim students.

It was a felony to have any contact with the PLO. Any such contact would get us expelled from the country, or worse. Furthermore, the PLO headquarters at that time was in Tunisia, North Africa.

All Palestinian colleges required a license from the Israeli military authorities. The authorities had granted a license to Bethlehem Bible College. We were able to get our visas through the Bible College.

We had no such license for our Friendship Center. The Israelis had shut down all Palestinian youth clubs in the West Bank and Gaza Strip. The Israelis were fully aware of our Friendship Center, but we had no license or permission to operate the Center.

The Israeli Authorities: It was my job to keep us on the good side of the military authorities. The military governor showed me a three-inch thick folder he had on us. In a very indirect way, he told me, "We know what you are doing. We do not want to interfere because it is something positive. Just don't ask for permission and don't come to our official attention."

He casually mentioned, "I understand you have a place of prayer in your building." I was going to respond with an explanation. Then I realized he was telling me something. He was choosing to view our Friendship Center as a religious place of prayer rather than as an illegal youth center. I said no more.

On another occasion, the military governor ordered us to appear in his office. I told Willow to wait in the hallway, while I went in to talk to the military governor. He was looking at my file when I entered. He said, "I see that you had some kind of altercation with the Village League."

The Village League was a failed attempt of the Israelis to create an alternative to the PLO. The Israelis recruited one family in each Arab village as their village league representative. Palestinians needing a permit or license had to apply through this representative.

The village league became a license to extort money and lord it over other Palestinians. Village League thugs had badly beaten Bethlehem University's gatekeeper.

I asked the military governor, "When did this alleged incident happen? He gave me the date. I told him I was out of the country, in America, on that date. I showed him the exit and entry stamps on my passport.

We both tried to figure what this report was about. We suddenly realized. "It was Willow!"

While I was out of the country, a Village League thug tried to prevent Willow from entering our apartment. Willow did not back down. The neighbors gathered in support of Willow. The thug had to back down.

The military governor and I had a good laugh at Willow's expense. Nothing further was ever said about this incident, and the Village League program quietly faded away.

The Palestinian Authorities: It was Willow's job to keep us on the good side of the PLO and other Palestinian factions. However, we could not contact them directly. She had to depend on word of mouth by locals to vouch for us to people whose identity we could not know. Willow learned many things that she was not supposed to know.

Neither the Israeli military nor the PLO ever interfered with our Friendship Center. Both sides were willing to maintain a diplomatic fiction that we had no contact with the other side.

Nor did they ever ask us for information about our contacts with the other side. We were very careful not to cross over the invisible lines of what was allowable by either side. We walked this tight rope every moment of every day.

We also had to consider the Muslim religious authorities in the community. It was only natural for them to be suspicious of foreign Christians discussing religion with their young people.

The first time I taught a class on Islam at the Bible College, several Muslim religious authorities asked to sit in on my class. They wanted to know what I was saying about Islam. After one session they went away, satisfied that I was teaching Islam correctly, and with proper respect.

Local Muslim authorities sometimes referred tourists to us who wanted to know more about Islam.

Meanwhile, I continued teaching at Bethlehem Bible College. I usually taught Old Testament, Biblical Geography, and comparative courses on Judaism and Islam.

The Biblical Geography courses were the most fun. We took our students to biblical sites in Israel they could not have visited on their own. We swam with them in the Sea of Galilee (Lake Kinneret), hiked in Galilean hills, and stayed in a hostel in Tiberius.

We also took some of our Muslim students on field trips. Willow took some to the Zoo near Tel Aviv. This is a safari type zoo where the animals roam free and visitors drive through in their cars. The students got out of the car and started chasing the animals across the fields. A guard came and chased them back into the car. No students or animals were eaten on this trip.

OUR BETHLEHEM FRIENDSHIP CENTER

By year's end, we had outgrown our facilities in Beit Jala. Our lease was up, so we started looking around for larger facilities.

We found a large new apartment building in Bethlehem, just down the hill, a "stone's throw" from Bethlehem University. Flying stones would soon become a part of daily life.

The building was diagonally across the street from the small `Aza refugee camp. A number of students from the camp became regulars of our new Friendship Center.

We were now more centrally located. It was much easier for students to drop in between classes at the university. 'Aza Camp students could simply cross the street to our Center. But we were also much more visible and exposed in times of conflict.

We leased three, and later five apartments in this building. These were spacious new three bedroom apartments. Our Friendship Center occupied the first floor.

We lived on the third floor. Our front balcony and windows looked east, out across the Judean desert and across the Dead Sea. On a clear night, we could see the lights of Jordanian villages on the cliffs above the Dead Sea in Jordan.

Willow decided to create a library of reference works where students could study after hours. I was doubtful if this was feasible, but she proved me wrong. She raised the money and got hundreds of books donated by universities in the USA.

Our Six Weeks guest worker and student internship programs were now providing a steady stream of short-term workers. This was a great help because I was splitting my time three ways: At "Baptist House" in Jerusalem, teaching at Bethlehem Bible College, and our Friendship Center.

RURAL VILLAGES AND REFUGEE CAMPS

With more help in the Friendship Center, we were able to spend more time in the refugee camps and rural villages. We always went as invited guests of Willow's former students.

Willow would often entertain the women and children with stories told with the help of hand puppets. We both told Bible stories. She also brought along needlework, which the ladies compared with their own needlework. Willow became an expert in traditional Palestinian needlework.

Palestinians—both Christian and Muslim—have a strong hospitality code. For example, a destitute traveler could always go to the nearest mosque and sleep on the carpet. Someone would see him there and arrange for a family to take him in for the night, or up to three nights.

The families always received us warmly, with true Arab hospitality. First, our hosts would serve us a cold drink. Then they would offer fruit or sliced vegetables. In winter, people would serve hot tea in lieu of the cold drink.

If a village family had nothing in the house to serve, they would get something from their neighbor. If the neighbor had nothing, the neighbor would go to the store and get something. Usually, though, we were expected, and the family was well prepared.

There was no escape for at least two hours. Finally, our hosts would serve coffee in a small demitasse cup. The coffee was very strong and flavored with ground carda-mom seeds.

After the coffee, we were free to leave. However, if this was near mealtime, there was no leaving until we had eaten with the family.

(Before we left Tacoma for the Middle East, we took a few Arabic lessons from a Palestinian-American woman in town. She was teaching us the polite rituals of coffee.

I asked her, "What should we say if we did not want any coffee?" She gave me a puzzled look and said, "You will drink the coffee. There is no refusing the coffee.")

A tense moment: Once, Willow was visiting with the women in the home of a Muslim Imam. (An Imam is the leader of a Mosque, much like the minister of a church). An Israeli army officer came to the door to talk to the Imam regarding an issue regarding the Mosque. The Imam stepped out on the porch to talk to the officer. The matter was resolved, and the Imam signaled to the women to bring out coffee.

The Israeli officer declined the coffee. There were several tense moments, while the Imam and the Israeli officer did not know what to do. The Imam interpreted the Israeli's refusal to drink the coffee as a disavowal of the agreement just reached.

An Orthodox Jew can set aside most Torah commandments in order to save a life. The Israeli officer decided that this was one of those times. He reached out, took the coffee, and drank it. Everyone relaxed.

Afterward, Willow explained to the Imam the kosher laws, which prohibited the Jewish officer from accepting the coffee from a non-Jew, and how to work around them when necessary.

Sheep's eye—yum, yum: Willow and I were guests at the Imam's home for the Feast of the Sacrifice (Id Al-

Adha). As the guest of honor, the Imam served me one of the eyes of the sheep. I swallowed it down quickly. I did not ask for seconds. Willow was happy to go without a sheep's eye. Discrimination is not always a bad thing.

The more typical village meal is rice served on a large platter with chicken piled on top. Sometimes cauliflower is first sautéed, and then cooked in the rice. We would all sit on the floor around the platter and eat with our hands. Some families offered us a spoon. A salad of finely chopped tomatoes and cucumbers, flavored with mint was a common accompaniment.

The meals with middle-class townspeople were more elaborate, with table, chairs, and individual dishes instead of the floor and a common platter. The meals would often include a mezza' of small salad dishes as well as the main dish.

Whether in the town or in the village, Christian or Muslim, Arab food is delicious and generous, and the hospitality is gracious and warm.

Often, a neighbor would learn of our visit. They would want us to visit them as well. A village visit sometimes turned into an all day affair. There was no such thing as just dropping by for a few minutes.

Our little blue car was perfectly safe in the villages where we visited. As soon as we arrived, the family would dispatch one of the children to watch our car. No one in the village would knowingly harm a guest's car.

Driving the rural roads was less safe because of our

yellow Israeli license plates. At first glance, village youths would assume we were Jewish settlers.

If we saw hostile looking youths by the roadside, Willow simply rolled down her window and waved her hand puppet. That was all it took. By this time, most of the villages where we drove recognized Willow's hand puppets.

When I was not with her, Willow would take a student as an escort and translator. Her student escorts would complain to me afterward of how terrified they felt at the time.

El Khader: This village was just down the road a couple of miles from Bethlehem. Our friends Mahmud and Ahmad lived in this village.

(Khader means "George" in Arabic.) What was notable about this Muslim village was the Greek Orthodox Church of St. George in the center of the town.

The church was abandoned for most of the year, except for a caretaker. But once a year, on St. George's Day, Christian Arabs from all around would gather at the church. The Muslim villagers set up booths around the church to sell food and souvenirs to the Christians. It was a very festive occasion.

Inside the church, bolted to the stone floor, is a set of chains and manacles. In ancient times, people brought mentally ill members of the family to this church. People believed that being in the presence of the holy monk of this church would drive away the evil spirits causing the mental illness. The mentally ill person was chained to the church by these manacles.

People were still bringing their children to this church. The parents would drape the chains around their children briefly as a good luck charm and preventative against illness.

The Muslim people of Al Khader proudly refer to St. George's Church as "their church."

Back to the village with the well: Seir was the village with the well mentioned in Chapter 2. Willow had determined to visit this village one day. The village is in a narrow valley about eight miles east of Hebron. Two of Willow's students were from this village.

We visited both families several times. We also attended one student's wedding in this village. Willow's dream of getting to know people of this village came true.

The village of El Shoukh: This village was even more remote than Seir. We had to go through Seir to get there. From Seir, the road climbed a long grade to the top of the ridge. This village was home to two of Willow's students, Hijazi and Ibrahim.

Ibrahim was one of Willow's first English students. He was a shepherd and farmer from a very poor family with a half finished house. Troubles at home forced Ibrahim to drop out of the university. His father died, his mother had crippling arthritis in both hands, and his two brothers were in prison. Ibrahim had to take over as provider and head of the family.

We frequently visited the three refugee camps in the Bethlehem area. We also made a number of visits to refugee camps in the Gaza Strip.

MEANWHILE, IN JERUSALEM

Willow and I enjoyed going into West Jerusalem on Saturday evenings after the end of Shabbat. We liked to sit in a sideway table at a cafe on Ben Yehuda street, sip a cup of coffee, and eat a dessert.

We continued to worship at "Baptist House" on Saturdays. I also served on the church pastoral council. When Pastor Bob Lindsay was out of town, I shared the preaching duties with a colleague, Dr. Wesley Brown.

I served several terms as Moderator of the congregation, and chaired the building committee, working with our Israeli architect after the church was burned down.

In 1987, Pastor Bob Lindsay retired and returned to the USA. The congregation and the other Baptist personnel in Israel asked me to step in as Interim Pastor.

It was no easy assignment. The congregation included "charismatics," "non-charismatics," and "anti-charismatics." There were strained relations between the congregation and the foreign mission board who owned the church property.

Messianic Jews worshipped along side of Christian Arab believers. A majority of the ex-patriot members were working on the Jewish side. Some served in the Israeli army. A few, like us, were working on the Arab side.

We were also in the midst of a fund raising campaign to replace the burned out building.

The Baptists regarded me, a non-Baptist, as a neutral third party. We were able to work through all these issues during my nine months as Interim Pastor. (These successes led me to become a professional mediator after we returned to Tacoma).

During this time, I took a course in Hebrew. Our co-worker Fred Mollon and I also studied Judaism at Hebrew University.

I was teaching Bible, Judaism and Islam to Christian Arabs at Bethlehem Bible College; Christianity and Judaism to Muslims in our Friendship Center, while continuing our relationships with our Jewish friends in Jerusalem.

Going back and forth between Jerusalem and Bethlehem, and working with Christians, Muslims, and Jews created a lot of dissonance for me. I was living and working in two very different cultures, on opposite sides of the conflict. The work was often intense and always stressful. They were also the most exciting and fulfilling times of our lives.

CHAPTER 5

A Time to Love

Many of Willow's earlier students had now graduated from the university. It was their time to marry and start a family. We were getting invitations to weddings.

One of our team members, Duane Rogers, fell in love with Karimah, a lovely Christian Palestinian woman. She was from a family in Beit Sahur and a schoolteacher. Karimah's younger sisters were students at the Bible College.

Willow and I sat with Duane at the formal engagement meeting as his "in locos parentis." However, long before the romance reached this stage, Karimah's two younger sisters were doing their sisterly duty by scheming and plotting to push the romance forward.

Duane does not have a sister, but our youngest daughter Deborah was staying with us at the time. Deborah served as Duane's surrogate sister. She schemed, and plotted on Duane's behalf with Karimah's sisters. (The men do not usually have a clue in such matters. They actually think that they are making all the decisions. Imagine!).

They were married in the Lutheran Church in Bethlehem. Karimah's family helped Karimah and Duane build a house in Beit Sahur. Duane continued to teach at Bethlehem Bible College and work in our Friendship Center.

Traditionally, a young man's family chooses a bride for him. The bride is usually from the same village. She is chosen from a family of an equal social standing. A man could marry down. A woman can marry up, but never marry down.

The theory is that a man, as provider for the family, can raise his wife to his social level. However, a wife can do very little that would raise her husband's social level if she marries down.

This strongly reinforces the idea of "family honor." Any behavior that detracts from "family honor" can negatively affect the marriage prospects of the entire extended family for generations to come. This serves as powerful constraint on individual behavior.

A Christian woman can marry a Muslim man. She can remain a Christian; her husband must allow her to attend church. However, the children will be considered Muslim.

A Muslim woman cannot marry a Christian man. For a Muslim woman, this would amount to apostasy. Professor Khalidi told me of a Muslim woman who fell in love with and married the U.S. vice-consul in Jerusalem. A diplomatic crisis was averted only when the U.S. vice-consul converted to Islam.

Courtship usually happens like this: The families arrange a meeting with the prospective bride and groom. The groom sits with his family on one side of the room; the bride and her family sit on the other side. The prospective bride and groom look at each other from across the room. Then it is decision time for the prospective couple.

In the villages, boys often marry at age 17 or 18. Girls are married as young as 14, but usually 16 or17. University study usually postpones marriage until after graduation.

Although families choose the brides for their sons, neither is forced into the marriage. Either the man or the woman can veto his or her family's choice. However, a son or daughter who declines more than two or three selections will come under terrific pressure from the family to "get a life." Love is not the basis for this choice. Marriage comes first; love comes later.

If the parties agree, they enter into an engagement contract. In Arab Christian marriages, there is no "bride price" involved. Instead, the father of the groom presents the father of the bride with an envelope containing a certain sum of money. The bride's father always refuses the envelope.

Bed Sheets and Bride Price: In Muslim marriages,

the "bride price" is essential. The engagement contract specifies the bride price to be paid by the groom. It is usually paid in gold jewelry and wedding dresses.

This does not mean he is "buying" his wife. Palestinian society is patrilineal and patrilocal. The bride will go to live with the groom and his family. The children are reckoned as members of the groom's family. (The idea that wives are "property" is a western invention, not an Islamic doctrine.)

The bride price compensates the bride's family for this transfer of members to the groom's family. The gold jewelry, kept by the bride, has sometimes served as a source of emergency funds in dire circumstances, such as when Palestinians were forced to flee their homes as refugees.

A traditional village wedding can cost as much as $10,000. In addition to the bride price, the wedding feast must be prepared, sometimes for hundreds of relatives and friends. (A feast may also be part of the engagement ceremony). Often the family rents a hall and hires an orchestra hired for the festivities.

Families would sometimes waive these expenses during hard times.

The wedding feast is held once the groom has paid the bride price. There is much dancing and ribald singing. The men and women dance separately.

In traditional times, the wedding party returned to the new husband's home after the feasting and dancing. The bride and groom retreated to a bedroom and consummated the marriage. The adult members of both families waited in the living room for the bride's cry indicating that that the marriage was consummated.

The groom would later present to the bride's father the sheet with its bloodstain proving that the bride was a virgin. Family honor was upheld.

The Old Testament refers to these bloody sheets as "tokens of virginity." (See Deut. 22:15).

We heard a story of a considerate groom who wanted to spare his shy bride the embarrassment of consummating the marriage with the families listening in the next room. He smuggled a vial of chicken blood into the wedding chamber. The bride gave the expected cry, and they went to sleep. The bloodstained sheet was duly presented to the girl's father, and honor was upheld. The couple consummated the marriage later, in privacy. The family regarded the husband as a romantic fool.

But we were told that the bloody sheets are no more. Instead, before the wedding, the groom's mother or aunt pays a visit to the bride's home and confirms the bride's virginity by physical examination.

Times are changing. Bethlehem University is now coeducational. Palestinian men and women are able to meet and socialize at the university.

From our window, we could see women students walking primly past our apartment to the university. They would be wearing an ankle length coat, with their head covered by a scarf or hijab. (Palestinian women do not usually wear a veil.) There would be no stopping to talk to boys along the way.

Once inside the walls of the university, off came the coat revealing fashionable jeans. She would pull out of her handbag high heels and lipstick. Now it was OK to talk to the male students. Going home after school, the process was reversed.

A young man attracted to a young woman can usually badger his family into selecting the girl of his dreams, if she is from a "suitable" family.

Our Social status: Even we, as foreign workers, had a certain social status in the Bethlehem community. My status grew as our team grew. I moved up a notch when Willow's mother came for a visit. When my parents came for a visit, I moved up another notch. Our daughter Deborah's arrival moved us up another notch.

With our full team of Fred and Ivy, Duane and Karimah, plus our short-term guest workers, I was treated as the patriarch of an extended family.

When short-term workers arrived, I would take them up to the market and introduce him or her to one of the moneychangers. They could then cash checks on their U.S. bank for whatever currency they needed.

The moneychangers and merchants knew that I would make good any bad check or credit problems. Business is conducted based on family reputation. If I did not make good any problem, our reputation would suffer, and it would become difficult to do business in Bethlehem.

We paid the rent on our five apartments every three months in U.S. dollars, in cash. I would simply walk up to the moneychanger in Bethlehem and hand him a check for $3000 drawn on our American bank. He would count out the cash, which I would give to our landlord. No identification was needed; no questions were asked. It was much easier cashing a check on a Tacoma bank in Bethlehem than in Tacoma.

Family reputation is everything in a Palestinian community.

Ibrahim's wedding: In Chapter 4, I described Ibrahim's village of El Shoukh. The wedding of Ibrahim and Samira was a joyful occasion in the village.

Willow served as the sponsor for the young couple. Ibrahim had no money to buy gold jewelry for Samira. Willow had some inexpensive gold plated costume jewelry she had bought at Woolworth's and J.C. Penney's. She gave the jewelry to Ibrahim for Samira. She cautioned Ibrahim and Samira they could not sell it as gold, since it was only gold plated. This saved face for both families.

We continued to visit Ibrahim and his family in their village. Ibrahim and Samira proudly brought their first baby to the Friendship Center for a happy visit.

CHAPTER 6

Intifada!

"Intifada" means "a shaking off." It is from the same Arabic verb Jesus used when he told his disciples to "**shake** the dust from their feet" when leaving an unresponsive town. (Matt. 10:14). The media usually translated intifada as the "uprising."

The Intifada began in the Gaza Strip in October of 1987. An Israeli truck ran down and killed four Arab workers waiting for their ride to work. Angry protests and riots broke out. The Israeli army fired into the crowds killing more Palestinians. This only served to spread the conflagration.

At the time we thought, "We're glad we are living in Bethlehem, and not Gaza." But that did not last long.

One morning we looked up toward Bethlehem University and saw a huge Palestinian flag flying over the campus. All the neighbors, including the people in the 'Aza refugee camp, were outside staring at the gigantic flag. Everyone knew something was about to happen.

The intifada had arrived in Bethlehem, with terrible effect.

THE SIEGE OF 'AZA CAMP:

The violence of the intifada quickly picked up momentum. The 'Aza Camp next door was frequently under siege by the Israeli army. Tear gas drifted into our apartments when the wind was from the north. At night, we often saw tracer rounds streaking up past our balcony.

Ishaq: The Israel army showed up and surrounded the university. One of our really nice Muslim students, Ishaq, stepped outside his classroom to go home. An Israeli sniper posted on a nearby rooftop shot him in the head. Ishaq died the next day.

We were all devastated. We had gotten very close to Ishaq. He was a kind and quiet boy, not an activist nor a terrorist.

School Closures: The Israeli military closed all the Palestinian schools, including Bethlehem University. Bethlehem Bible College continued to hold classes. The military chose to ignore the college, so we were able to graduate our senior students.

The next fall, the military informed us that the college would have to abide by the closure notice. We moved our classes to Tantur, a retreat and study center just inside

Jerusalem. In Tantur, we were no longer in the occupied territories; hence, we were no longer under military jurisdiction. The authorities made no objection. We were able to complete another school year and graduate our senior students.

The Israelis did arrest one of our Bible college students. After several weeks, the Israelis released him without charge. However, he was severely tortured in custody and required several surgeries to repair the damage.

Another Bible college student had his apartment building destroyed by the Israelis. A youth who threw a stone at an army jeep lived with his family on the first floor. Our student lived with his wife and child on the third floor. As punishment, Israeli soldiers destroyed the entire apartment building.

Later, some Israelis from a kibbutz came and helped rebuild the apartment building.

From Our Window: Willow and I had just sat down to lunch. Sounds of an angry crowd brought us to our window. We saw hundreds of people had packed the street from curb to curb. Many of these were women and children. They were marching and singing "Allah Akbar" (God is greater).

We saw the body of a man being carried overhead on a stretcher. The man had been killed several hours earlier. We learned later that he was the father of seven children and a resident of the Dehaishe refugee camp down the road.

Someone had fired a bullet at the camp from the Hebron road. The bullet went through his window, killing him instantly. The people of the camp were carrying him to the Muslim cemetery near Rachel's Tomb for burial.

A line of Israeli soldiers in battle gear confronted the marching, chanting crowd. Army helicopters throbbed and circled overhead. Jeeps and trucks with soldiers patrolled in front of and behind the procession.

The crowd continued to march toward the cemetery. The soldiers marched backward while facing the advancing crowd. Finally, the procession arrived at the cemetery. The man was buried and the crowd disbursed without further incident.

This time both sides exercised restraint in spite of the obvious tension and emotion. It did not always turn out this way.

Terror at Night: One night we heard screams from the camp next door. The loudspeakers on the nearby mosque were shouting, "God is greater, God is greater." The mosques in neighboring towns and camps picked up the cry.

We saw Israeli soldiers dragging the men out of their homes in the camp. They lined them up against a wall. We watched in horror as the soldiers began beating the men with clubs.

We saw a soldier club one man to the ground. The soldiers dragged him by his hair to a jeep and took him away.

Downstairs, our Friendship Center was full of our student friends. Several of them were from the camp next door. When they saw their brothers and fathers being beaten, they tried to rush out to help them. We locked the door and made them stay inside the Center.

The soldiers herded the men into a row of Israeli army busses and took them away. They were taken out a few miles into the desert and released to walk home in their pajamas.

One day we looked out our front window and saw a squad of soldiers. A boy about ten was walking down the sidewalk. We saw the soldier kneel down and take aim at the boy. We held our breath and prayed. Just then, an old man started down the street. The soldier looked up, and the boy ran safely away. The old man continued unmolested and the soldier moved on.

On still another occasion, two Christian Arab boys from up the street came to visit us. Soldiers came and blocked the streets around our Center. There was a lot of shooting and tear gas. There were a few moments of quiet, so the boys decided to go home.

Willow and I went out with them to walk them home. As we stepped outside, there were huge volleys of automatic fire. When the firing stopped, I said "Willow?" She said, "David?" We were surprised that we were both still alive. Neither we nor the boys were hurt. They scampered on home and we went back inside.

Duane and Karima's home was twice the target of

a bomb. First, a Jewish terrorist group called "terror against terror" placed a crude grenade bomb against their door. The police safely detonated it. A year or so later, a Palestinian threw a Molotov cocktail at a passing Israeli bus. The Molotov glanced off the bus and went through the window of their house. It landed and exploded in their children's bedroom. They were able to put out the flames and no one was hurt.

Duane and Karima's homes seemed to be "equal opportunity targets."

There were also a few lighter moments.

The case of the sinister red box: One day I glanced out our window and did a double take. A police car was blocking our street. I went out on our balcony for a closer look. I saw that police and soldiers were blocking off the cross street at the end of our building, as well as the street in front.

I saw a police sapper (bomb disposal) buckling on his protective gear. He pulled a kind of robot out of his van and started toward the restaurant at the end of our building. From our balcony, I had a glimpse of something red on the curb in front of the restaurant.

I watched as the sapper approached it with his radio-controlled robot. He then retreated to his van and fired the robot's gun. Pieces of something red flew everywhere. The detonator gun was the only explosion.

Later, around 2 PM, the Mollon kids came home from

school in Jerusalem. Christian was in tears. While waiting for the bus that morning, he had set his red lunch box down on the curb. When the bus came, he forgot to pick it up.

He did not discover his loss until he got to school. No sandwich, no thermos of chocolate milk. I took him out and showed him the few remaining fragments of his lunch box. We bought him a new one.

There were other comical incidents. One day, an Israeli soldier was driving by Duane and Karimah's house in Beit Sahur. Some kids started throwing rocks at the soldier's jeep. The soldier got out of his jeep and pointed his rifle at the children.

The rifle fell apart. Pieces fell on the ground. The soldier looked terrified and about to cry. Duane watched as the panicky soldier scrambled to pick up the pieces. The embarrassed soldier drove quickly away in his jeep.

The hamburger shootout: Hamburger can be hazardous to your health. I was on my way to the Bethlehem market to buy hamburger from my favorite butcher shop.

An army patrol was passing by just as I started up the steps to the market. Stones started flying from youths at the top of the stairs. The soldiers opened fire in both directions, up and down the street. I ducked into a nearby shop. No one was hit; I bought my hamburger, and returned home safely. Several weeks before, Fred had a similar experience. A week after my hamburger adventure, the same thing happened to Ivy and her daughter Sarah, on the same stairs.

We discussed this as a team. Willow said, "From now on, buy your hamburger at the Supersol in Gilo (a nearby Jewish settlement) or in Jerusalem."

Ivy and I both protested: "The hamburger in Bethlehem is much better and 2 shekels cheaper per kilo." (Moreover, probably lower in cholesterol.)

Willow then laid down the law: "You idiots! No more hamburger from the Bethlehem market. I forbid it!"

Facing our fears: Anyone who claims he is never afraid, is a liar, or lacks good sense. We were often afraid. A newsletter I sent home tells the story of just one night during the intifada:

It is getting dark. The sound of gunfire brings us to the window. We see that the camp children have blocked our street with stones. Orange flames leap from a burning tire in the middle of the road.

In the light of the fire, we catch glimpses of masked youths. They are ready to throw stones at any cars that try to run their stone barricade.

Israeli soldiers fire several more shots. The youths vanish into the dark alleys of the camp. The soldiers lob tear gas canisters into the camp after them.

An Israeli patrol ventures cautiously into the dark alley, fol-

lowed by a jeep with searchlights. We watch anxiously from our window and pray for the people caught up in this conflict.

Moments before, Willow had reminded me to take out the kitchen garbage. Now it was too late. The garbage bin is located in front of the camp entrance. The camp youths were using it as a shield while throwing rocks at the soldiers.

(Willow wondered why I didn't take out the garbage earlier, while it was still quiet).

Our Friendship Center became a safe house for Palestinian youths who wanted to stay out of trouble. Students kept coming to the Center even after the Israelis closed down all schools, including the University. They felt safer here than at home. In the Center, they could escape for a while from the storms of violence and fear that raged on outside. The Israeli soldiers did not interfere.

We tried to defuse some of the anger and bitterness that often leads to self-defeating and destructive activities. We listened while they talked out their fears and frustrations. We tried to live out Christ's call to be ministers of reconciliation.

But there was one sad exception:

Omar's story: Omar, one of our Muslim favorites, was arrested as a terrorist. We were devastated. What a waste of a promising young man's life!

Several times Willow took Omar's mother and sister to visit Omar in prison. She tried to be inconspicuous since we needed to keep a low profile with the authorities. But once, when she arrived at the prison, she locked her keys in the car. She told the guard at the gate, and he got a car thief out of the prison who unlocked her car for her. Inconspicuous? That's our Willow!

Omar was the only one of our Friendship Center students arrested as a member of a terrorist organization. (I have told Omar's story out of sequence, since it happened a year before the start of the Intifada.)

Out of contact: One consequence of moving from Jerusalem to Bethlehem was the loss of contact with our family and supporters in America. In Jerusalem, we had a telephone. In the West Bank, there was a seven-year waiting list for a telephone.

If one of us got into a bad situation, there was no way to call for help. We just had to deal with it. It made for some anxious waiting when a team member was out during outbreaks of violence.

Remember, this was the world before cell phones or the internet. To talk to our family back home we had to go to a neighbor willing to let us make a very expensive long distance call. The nine or 10-hour time zone difference made it difficult to arrange a time to call.

Mostly, we had to depend on the postal service. The problem was not getting mail from America to Israel. It was getting it delivered once it arrived in Israel. Airmail usually took about 10 days. Surface mail took two months or more.

We finally did get our own phone. A week later, the Israelis pulled the plug on all international phone calls from the occupied territories. As a result, we were once again cut off from our family back home.

Being out of contact with our family back home made it even more difficult to cope with an already difficult situation.

Our daughters back home would hear news reports of trouble and violence. But they had no way to find out if we were OK. Moreover, they had to do without the counsel or comfort of their parents.

LAST CHRISTMAS IN BETHLEHEM

December 1988: Many families in the Bethlehem area were mourning their dead or worried about their sons held in prison camps by the Israelis. The merchants in Bethlehem decided it would not be appropriate to put up the usual Christmas displays. There were few tourists coming anyway. There would only be the religious services in the churches.

The Israeli government did not want the bad publicity of no Christmas in Bethlehem. So Israeli soldiers arrived and forced the merchants to put up the usual Christmas displays.

Willow wrote a poem that expressed the deep sadness we were feeling that Christmas season of the intifada:

O little town of Bethlehem
Where shattered dreams and broken hopes
Lie rotting in the streets
Where screams are muffled by tinsel forced
And aching hearts in despair
Are left torn and empty in the night.
What happened to the babe of hope?
Or the light that shone so bright?
Where is the road
That leads to sparkling goals
And dreams about to be obtained
Yet perhaps in the stillness of the night
One might still hear a baby cry.
In spite of hate and soldier's feet
One can listen and hear a faint cry.
That cry of peace can still be heard.
O Little town of Bethlehem
In your silent night
May hope be born anew.

Meanwhile, we were trying to decide what to do about our usual Christmas feast for Muslims. We had already received our Christmas tree, but had not yet set it up. (The Israeli forest service supplied us with a Christmas tree each year topped from the Jerusalem forest.)

Willow asked a certain unnamed person what we should do. (The headquarters of the PLO at that time was Tunisia. As I said before, we were forbidden to have any contact with the PLO.)

We got back word from the PLO: "Please go ahead with your usual Christmas feast. It is the only bright spot for the people at this time." Of course, we have no idea how or from whom this word reached us.

We had our Muslim friends set up and decorate the tree. When anyone questioned our Christmas celebration, we just told them "so-and so" said it was OK. There were no more objections.

We did reduce our feast to one day. The crowd was a little smaller because it was too difficult for many of our regulars to travel in from their villages. But it was a special time of light shining in the night.

DECISION TIME

Crossing red lines: We knew we had to have an evacuation plan in the event that things blew up here. I had some mental red lines to help determine when it was time to go. But the red lines kept shifting.

We would cross a red line and I would think, "Well, this isn't as bad as I had imagined. We can cope with this." I would simply draw a new red line. As it turned out, we crossed a whole series of red lines.

Last trips to El Shoukh: It became too dangerous to drive to Ibrahim and Samira's village of El Shoukh with

Jewish license plates. So Ibrahim arranged for an Arab car and driver. Willow put on a village dress and a hijab on her head. (I thought she looked cute in it.)

She stayed overnight in the village and returned to Bethlehem the next day. Ibrahim, Samira, and their two small children escorted Willow home in the rented Arab car.

They dropped Willow off at our Friendship Center and headed back to their village. On the way back, Jewish settlers attacked their car. The settlers smashed out the windows of the car. Three-year-old Sabrina received a concussion and a cut from flying glass.

We realized from this and other incidents that we could not continue our village visits without endangering the people we were visiting. Nevertheless, Willow was determined to make one more visit to El Shoukh.

We knew Ibrahim could not work most days because of army blockages and closures. She decided to bring his family two 20-kilo bags of rice. One of our Muslim friends went along as an escort.

The roads were clear until she passed the village of Seir and started up the long grade toward El Shoukh. About half way up she came to a blockage of fire across the road. The youths maintaining the blockage wanted to push Willow and the car off the cliff.

She explained that she was taking rice to El Shoukh. She showed them the rice in the back of the car. The youths said, "Ok, we will go with you." They piled in the car and Willow drove on up to El Shoukh.

The village was expecting a new army blockade any moment, so Willow just dropped off the rice, and headed back with her escorts.

Halfway down the hill they came upon another fiery blockage. This one was "manned" by a ten-year-old girl. She asked one of the guys in the car, "When all this is over, can this lady come and tell me a story?"

A last trip to Gaza: This trip was not supposed to happen. Willow had been talking about going to Gaza to visit Muhammad, who lived in Bureij camp. I said, "No way! Not with what is going on in Gaza now."

I had to make a trip to Cyprus on business. I gave Willow strict orders to stay away from Gaza. As soon as I left for the airport, she set out for Gaza.

She knew she could not drive our car there, so she caught a taxi. She and a nurse shared the taxi to Gaza City. In Gaza City, she took a service taxi that runs between Gaza City and Rafat on the Egyptian border.

As they neared the turnoff to the Bureij camp, she told the driver to drop her off at the camp. The Arab driver stopped the car and told her: "I'm not going any closer to Bureij camp. Get out here!" Willow walked the rest of the way to the camp.

The Israeli army had bulldozed a high dirt bank around the camp. Willow scrambled over the bank and down into the camp. The streets were deserted, and she could not remember the way to Muhammad's house.

A young boy saw her walking and asked her where she was going. She told him, and he guided her there.

When she arrived, Muhammad said, "I just knew you were coming. There had been fighting for two weeks, and suddenly, everything became quiet." Willow stayed there several nights.

Meanwhile, back in Bethlehem, Fred was praying in a panic. In a few minutes, he was due to leave for the airport to pick me up. He dreaded having to tell me, "Willow went to Gaza and didn't come back."

At the last minute, Willow arrived home and Fred was off the hook. But Willow had just crossed one of my red lines.

A Strange Phone Call: Fred took the call as we were out at the time. The caller said he had a message for Willow. He said he could arrange for Willow to visit Omar in prison. He wanted to arrange a meeting with Willow at night. The caller had an American accent.

This was a very suspicious call. Willow could visit Omar at any time. She did not need any stranger to arrange it. A night meeting with some unknown stranger was just not in the cards.

As already mentioned, we were in a delicate position between the Israeli military, and the various Palestinian factions. We were determined not to allow ourselves to be used by either side against the other.

I suspected someone was trying to put Willow in a

compromising situation where she could be "turned" by one side or the other.

By this time, we had very good contacts on all sides of the conflict. We quietly made inquiries with our contacts. (Some stories still cannot be told.)

No one had any idea who was behind the call, but all agreed someone was trying to entrap Willow for no good purpose.

Meanwhile, the stress was beginning to take its toll on our whole team. Willow and I were both having medical problems. I had been diagnosed with type II diabetes. I was losing weight rapidly, and our doctors were not able to bring it under control.

Christian, now 9 years old, liked to play with the kids his age in the refugee camp next door. One day, Fred caught him throwing rocks at Israeli cars with the camp kids. That was definitely a no-no.

We had just crossed the final red line.

Decision time: It was definitely time to leave. Duane, Karima, and their two children had already left for the U.S.

Deborah flew in from the States to help us pack and get ready to leave. We had a sale of our personal furnishings and our faithful blue Ford Fiesta, now ten years old.

We turned the Friendship Center over to our friends, Charles and Elizabeth Kopp. We stayed with the Kopps in Jerusalem for our last several weeks in Israel.

The Mollon family stayed with some Mennonite friends in East Jerusalem. Mennonites believe in non-violence; they were appalled when Christian led the Mennonite kids into putting rocks across their street as a blockade.

One of those days, Willow and I stopped at an orange juice kiosk in Jerusalem for a drink. The Arab youth working in the kiosk told Willow: "I remember you. Don't you remember me? I was one of the guys who was going to throw your car over the cliff on the road to El Shoukh." (This was the first time I heard of this incident. Willow had not told me about it.)

Willow did not want to leave Palestine. She would have stayed if I had let her. She expressed her feelings in a poem she wrote during one of those dark intifada nights:

A Mother's Prayer

God, is there any chance you might hear me?
I live on the wrong side.
I pray in a different language than the others.
Today they tear gassed our camp
And we couldn't breathe.
I think one of the babies died.
Do you care?
My sons are in prison.
They didn't do anything.
They came in the night
And took them away;

Locked them away for six months.
I hear my youngest is sick.
No one can see him.
Do you care?
I have one son left.
I look out my window.
More soldiers are coming.
Will they take my last son?
God, do you even care?

We flew out together on the same plane with the Mollon family. We had a stopover in Copenhagen. From there, the Mollon family flew home to New York. We flew on to Seattle-Tacoma, arriving on November 2, 1989.

In Parts 2 and 3, I discuss what we learned in our years in Jerusalem and Bethlehem.

Part 2:
The Footsteps of Christ in Islam

*In their footsteps we sent Jesus son of Mary, fulfilling what was
revealed before him in the Torah. We gave him the Gospel containing guidance and light.* (The Quran, Sura 5:46)

*To this you were called, because Christ suffered for you, leaving you
an example that you should follow in his steps.* (1 Pet. 2:21)

*And you will find the nearest in friendship towards the believers in
those who say, "We are Christians."* (Quran 5:82)

Willow's Guys in the Friendship Center

CHAPTER 7

Muslim Followers of Jesus

We wanted our Muslim friends to know that Jesus is for Muslim people as well as for Christians. Jesus is our example of what it means to be in submission to God.

We gave our Muslim friends our love, acceptance, and friendship without condition. They shared with us their hopes and fears. They came to us in times of trouble. We prayed with them and together witnessed many gracious answers to prayer.

Our Muslim friends responded to our love and friendship. Many told us of a peace and hope they had found since coming to our Friendship Center. Some told us how Jesus had become more real and personal to them. They all appreciated that we were not trying to convert them and that we treated them and their Muslim faith with respect.

We were aware of the consequences for a Muslim who converts to another religion.

CONSEQUENCES OF CONVERSION

A Muslim who converts to Christianity will be disowned by his family and forced to leave his community. He will not be around to be a living witness of Christ to his own people. His family will be more embittered against Christianity for taking away a beloved son or daughter.

For a Muslim to lose his or her family is a double tragedy. In Arab societies, family solidarity is very important. Sons and daughters depend on their family to fund their education and obtain for them a marriage partner. Adult members work to support their aged parents, younger siblings, nephews and nieces.

Nor will the alienated convert find a ready welcome in a nearby Christian Arab church. The church will regard him with suspicion. They will suspect he is only pretending to be a Christian so he can marry a Christian woman.

Several pastors of Arab evangelical churches told us, "Please don't bring any Muslim converts to our church."

The consequences do not stop here. In the Middle East, there is not a "separation of Church and State" as we have in the West.

One's religious identity is a part of one's ethnic-national identity. Conversion involves far reaching legal and civil consequences. For a Muslim or Jew, becoming a Christian is not merely a matter of accepting Jesus and joining the church of one's choice. It amounts to a change in nationality.

We did not want to alienate our Muslim friends from their families. To quote David Fraser, "If Islam is to be evangelized; it will not be by the 'one by one extraction method that seems to be the present norm.'" (Fraser 1978)

In search of another model: We began looking for another model for our Friendship Center. We got some ideas from several recently published books and papers on Muslim evangelism.

One was Don Richardson's book, *Eternity in their Hearts.* (Richardson 1981) Another was Phil Parshall's books, *New Paths in Muslim Evangelism*, and *Bridges to Islam*. (Parshall 1981, 1983)

Charles Kraft had proposed the idea of a "Muslim-Christian" movement analogous to the movement of "Messianic Jews." There are Messianic Jews who accept Jesus as their Messiah while keeping Jewish Kosher laws. Some do not chose to identify as Christians. They prefer to keep their identity as Jews. He suggested this might apply to Muslim-Christians as well. (Kraft 1978)

With these ideas in mind, we decided to field test a new model, which we call: **Muslim Followers of Jesus.**

THE MODEL

In this concept, the Muslim follower of Jesus would not change his religion. He would not be considered a Christian. He would retain his Muslim identity, and remain a respected member of his family and community.

Is this concept possible? We decided to find out. Four questions came to mind:

1. Is it possible for a Muslim to follow Jesus and remain a Muslim? That is, without converting to Christianity?

2. What kind of spiritual process would this involve? What would being "born of the Spirit" mean in this context?

3. What minimum theological understanding would this involve? What Christian doctrines and practices would he or she need to believe and practice? What Islamic practices or beliefs must be left behind?

4. How would the Muslim follower of Jesus find nurture, corporate worship, and fellowship with others of like faith? What form might this take?

Our first task was to understand what it means to be a Muslim. That is the topic of the next chapter. Then we will take up the more difficult issues.

Before we proceed, I must make it clear that we never viewed our Muslim friends as experimental subjects. They were not study specimens. We cared about their well-being, invested in their future, and valued them as dear friends.

We learned from them much as they learned from us.

CHAPTER **8**

What Makes a Muslim a Muslim?

The words "Islam" and "Muslim" come from the Arabic root S-L-M, meaning "peace." Islam is the religion. A Muslim is a follower of Islam.

The word "Islam" means "submission" (to God). A Muslim finds peace in submitting to the will of God.

Islam's moral values include trust in God, sincerity, humility, resignation to God's will, keeping worldly ambition within decent bounds, giving good advice, contentment, generosity, hospitality, and social courtesy. (H. M. Khalidi 1979)

Islam has a set of devotional practices known as the "Five Pillars."

THE FIVE PILLARS OF ISLAM

1. **Confession:** One converts to Islam by reciting a simple creed with the intention of accepting Islam. That creed

is, "There is no god but Allah, and Muhammad is the messenger of Allah." Everything else can be learned afterward. A Muslim will hear and recite these words many times a day every day of his life, from birth to death.

2. **Prayer:** Devout Muslims pray five times a day. A call to prayer is issued from the Mosque. The first call to prayer is in the pre-dawn hour before sunrise. There are also prayers at noon, mid-afternoon, sunset, and before bedtime in the evening.

The nearest mosque to us was just across the street in the `Aza refugee camps. We would hear this call first. Then the fainter calls of more distant mosques would echo through the hills.

It was a beautiful sound, which we learned to love. It took us a while to get used to the 3 A.M. call. In time, we were able to turn over in bed and go right back to sleep. Now, living in Tacoma, we miss those sounds of the call to prayer. (It is possible to hear them on the internet, but it is just not the same.)

Before prayer, there is an elaborate ritual of washing. If there is no water available, rubbing with sand can be a substitute.

The Muslim faces Mecca throughout the prayer. The postures are standing, bowing, and kneeling with forehead touching the ground. The Muslim repeats these postures several times during the prayer.

The prayers include such phrases, as "Allah is greater," "God hears the one who praises him," and "Praised be my Lord," repeated several times. There is also a time for a personal petition or recitation of verses of the Quran. The prayer concludes with the benediction, "The peace and mercy of Allah be with you."

The Friday noon prayer is usually in the mosque. There is usually a sermon and/or a lengthy reading of the Quran with the prayers.

Other than at Friday noon, Muslims usually pray at home or even at work. Many Muslims carry a small prayer rug with them to their fields or place of employment. We designated a room at our Friendship Center for prayers and kept a prayer rug there for our Muslim students.

3. **Alms for the poor:** Muslims donate about 2½ percent of their annual income to the poor. Caring for the poor is highly stressed in the Quran. The alms one gives are not "charity." They are one's duty to God, who provides for the poor.

4. **Fasting:** This is a 30-day fast during Ramadan. The dates are governed by a lunar calendar. Ramadan occurs 10 days earlier each year by our solar calendar.

Muslims are not to drink or eat anything. This can be difficult in the summer, when workers must labor all day in the heat with nothing to drink.

The ban on eating and drinking ends at sundown. The fast resumes at dawn. Friends told us that a lot of food is consumed during these hours of darkness.

In Bethlehem, some cafes remain open during Ramadan to serve Christian customers. Any Muslim who slips in for a drink and a sandwich risks arrest if seen by a policeman. He will spend the rest of that day in jail.

Some of our Muslim students would sneak a snack from our Friendship Center refrigerator during Ramadan. We ignored such lapses.

5. **Hajj:** Once in a lifetime, if one's health and means permit, a devout Muslim should make a pilgrimage to Mecca. This is the high point of a Muslim's devotional life, and a cause for celebration when he or she returns home.

Islam applies these five pillars with a good deal of leniency. For example, a person may break the fast during Ramadan if he or she is ill or traveling. Pregnant women are also excused from fasting. The same applies to the required prayers. These can be made up later. Muslims are not expected to make the Hajj if it would create a severe hardship for their families.

In the Quran, God tells Muhammad not to be too hard on the people. God reminds Muhammad that He is compassionate and most forgiving.

These are the "five pillars." However, this is only the

beginning. Islam has rules and rituals that govern every aspect of life. There are moral considerations and polite sayings that go with every transaction and interaction in daily life, and even in one's more private and personal habits.

Jihad is sometimes discussed as a sixth "pillar." It means to "strive." There is a greater and a lesser Jihad. The greater Jihad is the internal struggle to overcome temptation and to bring one's mind and will into submission to God. The lesser Jihad is in the defense of the Muslim community.

BELIEFS

The basic beliefs of Islam include the following:

1. One God
2. Prophets and Messengers of God
3. Holy books
4. Angels
5. The Day of Judgment
6. Predestination

1. **One God:** Islam, like Judaism, is strictly monotheistic. Islam flatly rejects the Christian doctrine of the Trinity. To Muhammad, the three "persons" of the Trinity did not add up to one God.

Say not there are three gods. Desist; it will be the better for you.
Indeed, Allah is the only One God. God's holiness is not such that
He would have a son. (Sura 4:171)

(How many Christians outside of a Seminary under-stand all the Greek and Latin arguments over the Trinity and the human and divine natures of Christ?)

Some missionaries to African Muslims insist that "Allah" is not the Christian God. Some even refer to Islam's "Allah" as a satanic deception.

However, this is not the view of most Arabic-speaking Christians in the Middle East. "Allah" is the Arabic trans-lation of the Hebrew "Elohim." Christian Arabic bibles translate God as "Allah." I am comfortable using "God" or "Allah" interchangeably.

After all, our word "God" is itself a translation. It has its linguistic roots in some other religion and language, possibly Sanskrit or Farsi.

God in Islam is the creator and sovereign Lord of the universe. He is *"Lord of all the Worlds"* and *"Master of the Day of Judgment."* But God is also *"all merciful and compassionate to all."* (Khan 1970)

Muslims have 99 names of God, which they are en-couraged to memorize. These names describe the different ways of God in dealing with us humans. Many Muslims have a loop of 33 beads, which they use for meditating on God's names (much like a Catholic rosary).

These names do not define the essence of God, nor is God limited to these attributes. Muslims regard these as simply the most beautiful names of God.

Some of the frequently used names of God in the Quran include:

- *Al-Rahman* — "The Merciful to All."
- *Al-Rahiim*– "The Compassionate to Each."
  Al-Rahman and Al-Rahiim are sometimes translated "Most Gracious and Most Compassionate." Both of these expressions stem from a Semitic root meaning "tenderness." It is the root for the word "womb," both in Arabic and Hebrew.
- *Al-Ghaffur*– "The All Forgiving."
- *Al-Ghaffar*– "The Ever Forgiving."
- *Al- Katif*– "The Kind."

One Muslim teacher explained that Judaism reveals the **justice** of God. Christianity reveals the **love** of God. Islam reveals the **mercy** of God.

Of course, all three religions teach the justice, love, and mercy of God. The teacher was simply describing what he saw as the particular emphasis of each religion.

Islam does not emphasize the love of God. To say that God loves us implies to a Muslim that God is not self-sufficient. However, the Quran does describe God as *"Al Wadud,"* translated variously as *"Loving-Kind," "The Loving," "The Most Loving,"* and *"The All Kind."* (11:90; 85:14).

Instead, Islam emphasizes God's compassion, mercy and forgiveness.

This view of a merciful, compassionate, and forgiving God may not be the popular Western idea of Islam. Negative ideas about Islam are pervasive in our Western culture.

2. **The prophets and messengers of God:** Muhammad (Peace be upon him) is the prophet all Muslims revere as the final (or seal) of the prophets. His name means "praiseworthy." Muhammad is called a "Messenger" or "Apostle" of God.

   The title "Messenger" is given to prophets who received from God one of the Holy Books. These "Messengers" are Abraham, Moses, David, Jesus, and Muhammad. The Quran completed the revelation of God to humanity. No further Prophets or Messengers are necessary or expected.

   Muslims do not worship Muhammad as divine. He is simply a holy man selected by God to complete God's final revelation. Muhammad awaits the Day of Judgment like everyone else.

   Muslims often asked me, as a Christian, what I thought about Muhammad. I told them: "I respect Muhammad for his devout life and submission to God. It is not for me to judge the prophets or messengers of God. That belongs to God alone." This answer seemed satisfactory, as it is good Islamic doctrine.

Islam recognizes some 600 different prophets, including most of the prophets of the Old Testament. Islam views Adam as a prophet, as is Abraham, Isaac, Jacob, Moses, David, and Solomon. All of these biblical characters are considered to be Muslims. The Quran declares:

> *Affirm: We believe in Allah and in that which has been sent down to us and that which was sent down to Abraham and Ishmael and Isaac and Jacob and his children and that which was given to Moses and Jesus, and that which was given to all other Prophets from the their Lord.*
>
> *We make no distinction between any of them and to Him do we wholly submit ourselves.* (Sura 2: 136)

Muslims believe that God sent prophets to other nations, but these nations disregarded the message of the prophets.

Islam highly reveres **Jesus**. It is a grievous sin for a Muslim to disparage Jesus or use his name in a curse. I will elaborate on what Muslims believe about Jesus in Chapter 10.

3. **The Holy Books:** Muslims view Islam as a progressive religion. They believe that the revelation of God is contained in four Holy Books. There may have been a lost earlier book referred to as the "Scrolls of Abraham."

The four remaining books are:

- The Torah given to Moses
- The Book of David (perhaps the Psalms)
- The Gospel (Injil) given to Jesus
- The Holy Quran given to Muhammad

The first three of these books correspond to our Bible. Muslims are not prohibited from reading the Bible. However, they are not encouraged to do so, either. Muslims believe that the Quran contains the essentials of everything revealed in the previous Holy Books, so there should be no real need to read the Bible.

Islam teaches that God inspired the Bible, but Jewish and Christian interpreters have corrupted the text. This explains all conflicts between the Bible and the Quran.

Some of our Muslim friends did read the Bible. They had expected to find prophesies about Muhammad in the Bible. Muslims regard *"another prophet like Moses"* (Deut. 18), and the *"comforter/counselor"* promised by Jesus (John 14-16) as prophecies about Muhammad.

The Holy Quran: Muslims understand that Muhammad recited the verses of the Quran from an original text in heaven. The angel Gabriel came to Muhammad while he was meditating in a cave in the hills above Mecca. The angel told Muhammad: *"Recite: In the name of the Lord. He created everything! He created man from a clot of blood."* (96:2).

Muhammad protested that he was unable to read or write. However, the angel insisted, and Muhammad recited. Muhammad returned home in a state of shock. He was not sure what had happened to him. His devoted wife Khadifa wrapped him in a warm robe and reassured him.

Muhammad continued to receive these recitations as his movement grew and encountered new challenges.

Muhammad himself did not write the Quran. His followers memorized what he recited. Later, they wrote down what they remembered.

After Muhammad died, his followers collected these bits and pieces and organized them into the classical Arabic text that exists today.

Our Bible has a long history of development, with many contributors. There are many variations to our existing Hebrew and Greek texts. This is not so for the Quran.

There was just one preliminary draft written in the time of Caliph Uthman before the final version. All copies of the preliminary draft were then collected and destroyed.

There are no official or authoritative translations of the Quran. There are many unofficial English and other translations, of course. There are also several available on the internet. I have three in my personal library:

- Zaphrulla Khan's English-Arabic. (Khan 1970)
- Maulana Muhammad Ali's English Arabic. (Ali 1963)

- Tarif Khalidi's English (my preferred). (T. Khalidi 2008)

The chapter divisions of the Quran are called "suras." There are 114 suras. They are not arranged in chronological order. After the short opening sura, they are arranged in order of length, with the longest first.

The opening sura is called, "Al Fatihah." It is a beautiful prayer, which Christians, as well as Muslims have prayed:

In the name of God,
Most gracious and ever merciful.
All praise belongs to God alone,
The Lord of the universe,
Most gracious, ever merciful.
King of the Day of Judgment.
You alone do we worship;
To you alone do we direct our petitions.
Guide us in the straight path—
The path of those upon whom
You have bestowed your favor
Not as those with whom you are displeased
And those who have gone astray.

Later sayings in the Quran may supersede some earlier sayings. Without knowing the chronological order, it is uncertain which sayings still apply. The subheading of each sura tells only whether the sura was revealed in Mecca or Medina.

Interpreting the Quran requires scholarship beyond my meager knowledge of Arabic and Islam. I had to rely on my Muslim friends and teachers and the commentaries available to me during my studies to get this far in my understanding.

Christian opponents of Islam sometimes take verses in the Quran out of their historical context to picture Islam as a warlike and fanatical religion. Of course, critics of Christianity often do the same with the Bible. (This will come up again in Chapter 14.)

Judaism, Christianity, and Islam all have their extremists who use scriptures to justify ideologies of fear, hatred, and violence, ignoring the high moral teachings of their religion.

While the Quran is the primary source of Islamic teaching, there are other sources of lesser authority as well. In Sunni Islam, the order of authority is as follows:

- The Holy Quran
- The Hadith – traditional sayings by Muhammad not included in the Quran but attested to by a chain of witnesses. This is a much larger volume of literature than the Quran.
- The Sunna – The personal example and practices of Muhammad
- Consensus of the four traditional schools of Sunna Islam

4. **Angels:** Angels play an important role as messengers and executors of God's will. They do not have free will. There are also pre-human creatures called "Jinn," which were created from fire.

Muslims may call persons with a fiery temper (or red hair) a "Jinn."

Satan (sometimes called Iblis or Devil) is not an angel; the Quran describes him as *"of the Jinn."*

The Quran has a story of God's intention to create the man Adam. God tells the angels that he is giving Adam authority over the earth. The angels are to submit themselves to Adam.

The angels were concerned that Adam's children will be violent and will murder one another. However, God told the angels, *"I know what you do not know."*

The angels comply with God's command. They bow down in submission to Adam. But Satan refuses to submit. He tells God, *"I was created from fire; the man was created from dust. I am better than he."*

God tells Satan: *"You are of the Jinn and a disbeliever."* Satan is cast down from his status and confined to earth for the purpose of "testing" humanity.

Arabs may call a clever, tricky opponent a "Satan."

The Quran mentions both the angels Gabriel and Michael. Gabriel was the angel who brought Muhammad his first recitation of the Quran. As in Luke's Gospel, Gabriel was the angel who told Mary she would bear a son—Jesus.

5. **The Day of Judgment:** No one is immune from God's judgment, not even Muhammad. The comfort and pleasure of paradise awaits those who find favor with God. The fiery torment of hell awaits those determined by God to be among the wicked. Only God knows one's destiny. God will reveal that destiny on the Day of Judgment.

The Quran pictures **Paradise** as a garden watered by underground streams. However, most educated Muslims understand that descriptions of paradise are metaphors of the joys of dwelling in God's favor and presence. *"The greatest of all is God's good pleasure."* (9:72) I discuss this garden in more detail in Chapter 11.

(The off-quoted idea of 72 virgins awaiting suicide bombers in paradise is not a traditional Islamic teaching. This idea comes from a disputed interpretation of an obscure and questionable Hadith. It is religion perverted to serve a political agenda.)

Hell is a place of punishment. However, these punishments have a corrective purpose. Those who reject God's mercy and grace in this life will learn in hell the lessons they had failed to learn in life. Hell will purge them of these errors.

To the wicked, the torments of hell may seem eternal. Except for God's mercy, the torments of hell would be eternal. However, God's mercy encompasses all. One of my teachers explained: "Eventually, the winds of God's mercy will blow through an empty hell."

6. **Predestination:** Muslims believe that God determines Man's destiny. This is inherent in the very meaning of Islam—submission to God.

But this is not a passive fatalism. A Muslim is expected to work hard, make wise decisions, and do his best to better himself. Then he must finally accept the outcome, which only God will determine.

Every commitment the Muslim makes is conditional upon God's will. Everything is "Inshallah" (as God wills).

Are you going to sell your goat tomorrow at the market? "Inshallah! If this does not happen, it must not have been God's will. Otherwise, it would have happened.

We should not be too upset if the goat does not get to the market. Surely, you cannot expect anyone to do anything God has not willed.

"Inshallah" is written on the back window of Arab taxis. Will you get to your destination? The answer is "Inshallah." Will you get there on time? That too is "Inshallah."

This takes some getting used to for clock watching literal minded Westerners like me!

Free will: Islam also teaches that we have free will. We make moral decisions and God holds us accountable for those decisions. Some sects of Islam place more emphasis on predestination, others on free will. The greater emphasis is on predestination.

These are the basic beliefs of Islam. In the course of our many conversations, other issues came to light. These issues prevent Muslims from becoming Christians. They also prevent devout Christians from becoming Muslim. We will look at the most difficult of these issues in the next Chapter.

ISLAMIC SECTS

As with Judaism and Christianity, Islam has its different sects and divisions. The major division is between Sunni and Shi'ite Muslims. The Sunnis make up the majority of Muslims.

There are many sects within Sunna Islam. For example, the ultra-conservative Wahhabi sect is very influential in Saudi Arabia. Hamas in Gaza is a spin off from the Egyptian brotherhood, a fundamentalist movement of social reform.

My teachers and informants were all mainstream Sunni Muslims. My understanding of Islam reflects this Sunna interpretation.

The Iranians are Shi'ite Muslims. The Shi'ites broke off from the mainstream Sunnis after the death of Ali, the fourth Caliph or successor of Muhammad. The Shi'ites believed that a descendent of Muhammad should lead the

Muslim community. Iraq, Lebanon, and Syria have mixed Shi'ite and Sunna populations.

The basics of Islam are the same throughout the Muslim world. Some sects are more liberal, some more conservative. Many of these divisions are ethnic and political rather than theological, as Islam has spread throughout the world under different historical empires. Those details are beyond the scope of this book.

CHAPTER 9

The Difficult Issues

In our Friendship Center, we tried to correct any misconceptions our Muslim friends might have about Christian beliefs. In turn, our Muslim friends were eager to correct our mistaken ideas about Islam. We all had a lot to learn.

The most difficult theological issues involved:

- The Trinity
- The Sonship of Jesus
- Human Nature and Sin
- Redemption and the Cross

These doctrines stand as a wall separating Christianity from Islam. This same wall separates Christianity from Judaism as well.

THE TRIUNE GOD

For Muslims, the formula "God the Father, God the

Son, and God the Holy Spirit does not add up to one God. Our Muslim friends thought that the Christian Trinity consists of three gods—Jesus, Mary, and God. This idea comes from several passages in the Quran:

> *And when Allah will say: O Jesus, son of Mary, didst thou say to men, Take me and my mother for two gods beside Allah? He will say: Glory be to Thee! It was not for me to say what I had no right to say.* (5:116)

> *Certainly they disbelieve who say "Allah is the third of three."* (5:73)

> *And say not "three." Desist! It is better for you.* (4:117)

We assured them that we did **not** believe in three Gods. Nor that Mary, Jesus, and God make up the Christian Trinity. I tried to explain what we do believe about the relationship between God, Jesus, and the Holy Spirit.

I shared with them my own personal relationship with God. My parents were divorced. As a child, I hardly saw my biological father.

We pointed them to the Psalm: *"Though my father and mother forsake me, the Lord will receive me."* (Ps. 27:10) I told our Muslim friends that God is able to fulfill all of our needs. He can be a father to the fatherless and a mother to the motherless.

God has always been to me a wise and loving Heavenly Father, filling a role that was missing after my parents divorced.

I explained that we are all God's children, created to live in God's presence forever. Jesus told his disciples: *"I am returning to my Father and your father; my God and your God."* (John 20:17)

I explained how I see in Jesus the dutiful Son in perfect submission to God the Father. Jesus was to me the older brother I never had. In following Jesus, I know that I am on the *"straight path"* of submission to God that leads to eternal life.

When I go astray—and this happens—Jesus guides me back to the straight path and reassures me of God's forgiveness.

I talked about how the Holy Spirit enlightens me when I read the Holy Scriptures. When I pray, the Spirit guides my prayer. When I need wisdom, the Spirit is my counselor. All of this is the work of one God, who is all and all to me.

One of our Muslim guys did come up with an interesting analogy of a triune God. He used the example of the sun:

He said: "If I asked: 'What is that bright disk of light in the sky? You would say: 'It is the sun.'"

"If we went inside and I asked you: 'What is that shaft of light with the dust mites reflecting in it? You would say, 'It is the sun.'"

"If I then asked you: 'What is that oval of light on the floor at the end of the light shaft? You would say, 'It is the sun.'"

"There is only one sun but we see it in different ways."

THE SONSHIP OF JESUS

This issue revolved around two Arabic words for "son"—*Walid* and *Ibn*. Muslims would say to us, "You Christians believe that Jesus is *Walid Allah* (Son of God)." I would always insist, "No! Not *'Walid Allah.'* We believe Jesus is *Ibn Allah* (Son of God)."

The Arabic New Testament always speaks of Jesus as *"Ibn Allah,"* not *"Walid Allah."*

Ibn (like Ben in Hebrew) comes from a root "to build" (as in building up the family line). It is used both literally and figuratively.

Walid, on the other hand, comes from the root "to beget." Muslims often quote the passage in the Quran: *"God neither begets nor is begotten."* (Sura 112: 3) "Walid" usually means a boy child.

To say that Jesus was *"Walid Allah"* implies to a Muslim that God took Mary as a "consort" and had physical relations with her. That idea is blasphemous (to us as well as to them). We assured our Muslim friends that we do not believe that God had a physical relationship with Mary.

I asked our Muslims friends, "If I were to call you 'Sons of Palestine,' which word would I use? **Walid** Palestine? Or **Ibn** Palestine?" They would tell me, "**Ibn** Palestine."

I used this as an example of Ibn, which does not imply any consort or physical union.

We explained that the Bible uses *"beget"* both literally and figuratively. In Hebrew scripture, a midwife is called a *"begetter."* She *"begets"* the newborn child by bringing him forth from the womb. *"Beget"* in this idiomatic sense means "to bring forth."

(Exo.1:15-21)

Beget is also used in the installment of a new king in ancient Judah. In Judah, the elderly king would designate one of his sons to be his heir and regent. King David set this precedent in appointing Solomon as his successor. In the history of Judah, the retired king continued behind the scenes to mentor the young king, but the young king was now in charge.

Psalms 2 gives us the legal formula for this transfer of authority from the elderly king to his chosen son:

> *The LORD said unto me, Thou art my Son, this day have* **I begotten** *thee.* (Ps. 2:7 KJV)

Those who had business with the throne were advised: *"Kiss the son lest he be angry and you should be destroyed in your way."* (Ps. 2:12).

The gospels twice apply this royal formula to Jesus. The first time is at Jesus' baptism:

> *The Holy Spirit descended on him in bodily form like a dove, and a voice came from heaven,* **"You are my Son,** *whom I love; with you I am well pleased."* (Luke 3: 22).

The second time is at Jesus' mountaintop transfiguration: The three disciples heard a voice from the cloud: **"This is my Son,** *whom I have chosen; listen to him."* (Luke 9:35)

In both instances, the Father is declaring from heaven that Jesus is his chosen Messianic King. The Son is now in charge of the Kingdom of God on earth. God tells the disciples (and us): *"Listen to him!"*

The apostle Paul used "beget" to refer to the regenerating work of the Holy Spirit in the life of believers:

> *"...for in Jesus Christ I have begotten you through the gospel."* (1 Cor. 4:14 KJV)

> *"I beseech you for my son Onesimus, whom I have begotten in my bonds."* (Phile.10 KJV).

I used these examples to explain how the Bible uses *Son* and *begat* in a figurative way. It does **not** imply that Jesus was the product of a physical union between God and Mary.

Why does the Quran dispute this? Perhaps in Muhammad's time unlearned Christians in Arabia were using "beget" in a literal way. If so, the Quran would stand as a necessary correction.

We affirmed with the Quran that Jesus was conceived by the Holy Spirit. However, our Muslim friends did not accept the idea of Jesus' dual human and divine natures.

The church councils of the 4th and 5th centuries settled the issue of Jesus human and divine nature for Western Christians.

However, Coptic and Nestorian Christians were still debating these issues in the time of Muhammad.

Muhammad wanted to distance his followers from this

controversy. This may explain the statements in the Quran that deny Jesus as "Walid Allah" and of a divine nature.

At least we were able to reassure our Muslim friends on several points: Jesus was not born of a physical relationship between God and Mary. We do not believe in three gods. Jesus was a man of flesh and blood, who walked in perfect submission to the will of God. In other words, Jesus was an ideal Muslim.

What Muslims themselves believe about Jesus is the topic of Chapter 10.

HUMAN NATURE AND SIN

Islam and Judaism both reject the Christian doctrine of "original sin"—that human nature was corrupted by Adam's "fall," and that all of humanity has inherited Adam's sinful nature.

Islam and Judaism both see human nature as essentially good. Human nature did not change because of Adam's sin. Human nature remains exactly as God created it.

The religion of Islam is considered to be in perfect accord with our human capabilities:

> *So set your face to the Faith, and thereby follow the nature designed by Allah, the nature according to which he has created mankind.* **There is no altering the creation of Allah.** *That is the true religion, but most people know it not.* (30: 30)

Islam teaches that God has revealed the right way; it is

our choice whether to believe and obey, or disbelieve and turn away. God has given us the capacity to do either.

> *We have made him hearing and seeing; and we showed him the Way. He is either thankful, and follows it, or is ungrateful, and rejects it.* (76: 3)

Sin: Islam recognizes that humans commit sin. We are prone to lapses and forgetfulness. God sent prophets to remind people of their duties to God. But many turn a deaf ear to God's instruction:

> *Corruption has appeared on land and sea in consequence of people's misdeeds, that Allah may afflict them with punishment for part of their misconduct, so that they may turn back from evil.* (30: 42)

In this passage, it is human society, with its many religions, that is corrupted. Human nature itself remains unchanged.

Adam and Eve: The Quran has a story of Adam and Eve's sin in the Garden.

> *Satan made them slip from (God's commandment) and caused them to depart from the state they were in.* (2:36)

(Satan) said: *O Adam, shall I lead you to the tree of immortality and a kingdom that decays not? So they both ate of it. Then their evil inclinations (nakedness) became manifest to them and they began to cover themselves with the leaves of the garden. So Adam disobeyed his Lord and was disappointed.* (20: 120-122).

God confronted Adam with his sin and Adam acknowledged his wrongdoing.

They said: *Our Lord, we have wronged ourselves; and if you forgive us not, and have not mercy on us, we shall certainly be of the losers.* (7: 23)

God forgave Adam and Eve for their sin. God *"chose him and turned to him and guided him."* (20:122)

The consequences of sin: God is most forgiving but sin does have consequences. In yielding to Satan, Adam and Eve were *"caused to depart from the state they were in, and were disappointed."*

Earth became a place of "testing" for Adam and his descendents. They must now deal with thorns, weeds, and wild animals. Enmity would abound as population increased. Adam and all of his children are destined to die. God ordains the day of each person's death.

As noted in Chapter 8, God intends for his punishment to be corrective— *"so that they may turn back from evil."*

REDEMPTION

Islam rejects the idea that God requires a sacrifice in order to forgive sin. He is most forgiving and ever merciful. God forgives whom He wills.

Blood sacrifices for sin are neither necessary nor effective. *"Not their flesh, nor their blood reaches Allah."* (22:37).

In Islam, no one, not even Jesus, can atone for another's sin:

> *No soul earns but against itself. Nor does a bearer of a burden (of guilt) bear another's burden.* (6:164; 35:18)

> *We have made every man's actions to cling to his neck, and we shall bring forth to him on the Day of Resurrection a book which he will find wide open. Read your own book. Your own soul is sufficient as a witness against you this day.* (17:13-14)

The cross of Christ: Islam sees no redemptive purpose of Jesus' death on the cross. In fact, most Muslims do not believe that Jesus actually died on the cross. They do not believe that God would allow the righteous messenger Jesus to suffer such an ignoble and horrible death. This belief stems from the following passage in the Quran:

> *And as for the (Jews) saying: We have killed the Messiah, Jesus, son of Mary, the messenger of Allah, they did not kill him. Nor did they cause his death on the cross, but he was made to appear to them as such.*

> *And certainly those who differ therein are in doubt about it. They have no certain knowledge about it, but only follow a conjecture, and they killed him not for certain.*

> *Nay, Allah exalted him in His presence. And Allah is very Mighty, Wise.* (4: 157,158)

Muhammad had said that Jesus was the Messiah. Perhaps Jews in Medina were scoffing at this claim. They may have said that Jesus was no Messiah, since he was executed as an evildoer. Muhammad told them they were speaking out of ignorance.

Some Muslims explained that the Jews were confused and crucified someone else in Jesus' stead. Perhaps Judas; he certainly deserved it.

Jesus' death and resurrection: Muslims believe that everyone, including Jesus and Muhammad, is destined to die. It is not so clear exactly when Jesus died or will die:

> *Remember when Allah said: O Jesus, I shall cause you to die and exalt you into my presence...* (3: 55)

> *(The baby Jesus) then said: Peace on me the day I was born, the day that I die, and the day that I am raised to life.* (19:33).

> *I was a witness to them (the disciples) as long as I was with them, but when you caused me to die, it was you who watches over them.* (5:117).

Some Muslims say that Jesus was taken down from the cross while still alive, was secretly revived, and died a natural death some years later.

Others say that Jesus was taken up to heaven alive after his near crucifixion. He will return to earth in the last days to defeat the Anti-Christ. At that time he will die and be raised again in the general resurrection.

Muslim eschatology seems to me to be no less difficult than Christian eschatology.

The Cross, so central to our Christian faith, remains a stumbling block to Muslims, just as it was to the Jews and Greeks of biblical times. The cross has historic negative associations for Muslims, as it has for Jews. It does not help that the ravaging Crusaders flaunted the cross on their banners.

We were able to clear up many misconceptions. But we were not able to convince our Muslim friends on every issue. We will discuss this more in chapter 12.

First, let us consider what Muslims already do know about Jesus.

CHAPTER **10**

Jesus and Islam

Chapter 9 explains what Muslims do **not** believe about Jesus. In this chapter, we discuss what Muslims **do** know and believe about Jesus.

Jesus is a well-known and revered figure in Islam. The Quran says of Jesus:

> *In their footsteps we sent Jesus son of Mary, fulfilling what was revealed before him in the Torah. We gave him the Gospel containing guidance and light.* (5:46)

The Quran quotes Jesus as saying:

> *I am a servant of Allah. He gave me the Book (Injil=Gospel) and made me a prophet. He has made me blessed wherever I may be. He has charged me with prayer and almsgiving all my life. He has made me dutiful to my mother. He has not made me arrogant or graceless.*

Peace be upon me the day I was born, the day that I die, and the day I will be raised to life.

Such is Jesus son of Mary. (19:30-34)

The Quran speaks of Jesus as:
- The Messiah
- Conceived by the Spirit; born of the Virgin Mary
- A sign to humanity and a mercy from God
- A Word from God and the Word of God
- A Spirit from God
- A prophet and messenger (apostle) of God

`Issa is the Islamic Arabic name for Jesus. It is a popular name among Muslims. We had several `Issas in our Friendship Center fellowship.

THE BIRTH OF JESUS

The Quran affirms the virgin birth of Jesus by the Holy Spirit:

Remember also she who preserved her chastity, so we breathed into her of our Spirit and made her and her son a sign for humanity. (21:91)

The Quran beautifully tells the story of Jesus' birth. (3:45-49; 19:9-25)

The story begins as in Luke's gospel with the story of

Zachariah and the birth of John the Baptist (John is called Yahyah in the Quran).

The angel Gabriel then appears to the Virgin Mary. She does not recognize him as an angel at first, and is afraid that he intends to do her harm. She declares herself to be under the protection of God.

Gabriel assures her he means no harm; he is only bringing her a message from God. Mary would give birth to a "pure son." His name will be Jesus. *"He will be worthy in this world and in the hereafter, and of those who are drawn nigh (to God)."* (3:45)

Mary asks how this is possible, since she is untouched and chaste. Gabriel tells her *"Your Lord says, 'It is easy for me. We will make him a sign to humanity and a mercy from us.'"* (19:21)

Mary's time comes to deliver her child. She withdraws into a solitary place. Wracked with labor pains she grabs on to a palm tree. The pains were so severe that she wishes she had already died.

But a voice tells her of a stream flowing beneath her and of ripe dates on the tree above her. She is told to eat the dates and drink the cool water. She revives and gives birth to baby Jesus.

Later, she returns to her village carrying the baby Jesus. The villagers criticize her for having a baby out of wedlock.

The baby Jesus suddenly speaks up in defense of his mother. He declares that he is indeed a servant of God and a prophet, and God has given to him the Book (the Gospel).

STORIES AND SAYINGS OF JESUS

Sayings and stories of Jesus are scattered throughout the Quran, Hadith, and other Islamic writings.

Tarif Khalidi lists 303 sayings or stories of Jesus in Muslim literature, some as late as the 18th century. I highly recommend this book for a glimpse into what Muslims have thought about Jesus. One of my favorite stories follows:

> The man said (to Jesus), "How can a servant be truly pious before God? Jesus replied, "The matter is easy. You must truly love God in your heart and work in His service, exerting all your effort and strength, and be merciful toward the people of your race as you show mercy to yourself."
>
> He said, "Teacher of goodness: Who are the people of my race?" Jesus replied, "All the children of Adam. And that which you do not wish done to you, do not do to others. In this way you will be truly pious before God." (T. Khalidi, The Muslim Jesus 2001)

Within this story, we can hear echoes of Jesus' Great

Commandment, the Golden Rule, and the story of the Good Samaritan.

Stories of Jesus picture him as a Muslim prophet, moral teacher, eschatological figure, and ascetic holy man. Most Muslims believe Jesus is alive up in heaven. He will one day return to earth to defeat the Anti-Christ.

Ironically, it is easier for Muslims to believe in Jesus' resurrection, ascension to heaven, and second coming, than to believe that he died on the cross for our sins.

Later Islamic writings picture Jesus as an ascetic holy man. He renounces possessions and pleasures, and identifies with the poor. These later writers admired Jesus for his gentleness, humility, and compassion for the poor and suffering.

Muslim writers continued to create stories and sayings of Jesus for many centuries after the time of Jesus and Muhammad. Although these stories are imaginary, they testify that the figure of Jesus still inspires Muslim people.

CHRISTIANS IN THE QURAN

Christians and Jews are "People of the Book" in the Quran. They are the people who received the Torah and the Gospel. They enjoy a protected status under Islamic law. *There shall be no compulsion in religion.* (2:256)

Muslims have a high regard for Jesus. But their feelings about Christians and Jews are not so positive. Jews receive the harsher treatment. No doubt this reflects Muhammad's bad experience with the Jewish tribes in Medina, who took the side of the Meccans when the Muslims were under attack.

Obviously, the on-going Israeli-Palestinian conflict has inflamed these negative feelings.

Muslims are warned against trusting either Jews or Christians as their allies.

> *O believers, take not the Jews and Christians for friends (allies). They are friends of each other.* (5: 51)

> *You will find that the most hostile of people to the believers to be the Jews and idolators.* (5:82)

> *The Jews say that the Christians count for nothing; the Christians say that the Jews count for nothing, while they recite the same Book. Those who have no knowledge repeat these statements.* (2:113)

However, the Quran notes some exceptions:

> *They are not all alike. Of the People of the Book there are those who are upright. They recite God's messages in the night and bow low to Him.* (3:113)

> *Surely those who believe and those who are Jews and the Sabians and the Christians—whoever believes in Allah and the Last Day and does good—they shall have no fear nor shall they grieve.* (5:69)

Some of our Muslim friends pointed out to us this passage from the Quran:

> *And you will find the nearest in friendship towards the believers in those who say,"We are Christians." That is because there are priests and monks among who do not become proud."* (5: 82)

According to the Quran, Christians and Jews would be fine if only they took seriously and followed their own scriptures:

> *And if the People of the Book had believed, it would have been better for them. Some of them are believers, but most are disbelievers.* (3:110)

> *And if the People of the Book had believed and done their duty, We would certainly have removed from them their evils, and made them enter gardens of Bliss.* (5: 65)

The Quran sometimes has Jesus correcting some of the claims of his Christian followers:

> *And when Allah will ask: O Jesus, son of Mary, did you say to people take me and my mother as two Gods in addition to Allah?*

> *He (Jesus) will say, "Glory be to You! I would not say what I had no right to say. If I had said it, you would have known it, for you know what is in my mind. (5:116)*

Our Muslim friends knew us as Christian believers and followers of Jesus. We were happy to be considered their friends.

The footsteps of Christ in Islam: Jesus has made a deep inprint in the heart of Islam. He is seen as an example to follow of Islamic submission, morality and spirituality. That spirituality is the topic of the next chapter.

The Bible and the Quran both attest to Jesus as *"exalted in God's presence."* In John's gospel Jesus tells us: But I, when I am lifted up from the earth, will draw all men to myself. (John 12: 32).

The exalted Christ is exerting an upward pull on all of humanity. Muslim people feel that pull as do we. But fear and enmity can weight us down.

We yield to this upward pull when we yield to the love of Christ, who calls us *to love our neighbor as ourselves; to even love our enemies. For perfect love casts out all fear.*

As Christians, our team has endeavored to follow in the footsteps of Jesus. These footsteps have led us to Bethlehem, and into the hearts of our Muslim friends.

CHAPTER 11

Muslim Spirituality

Many Christians I've talked to see only the outer side of Islam. But Islam has a deeper, spiritual dimension for those Muslims who seek inner peace in submission to God. Here again I see the footsteps of Christ.

I like to use the metaphor of a walnut to discuss the outer and inner layers of any religion. (I can't recall who first used this metaphor.) The walnut has four layers—an outer husk, a hard shell, the nutmeat, and the oil.

The outer husk of Islam is what most Westerners see. In the shopping mall we often see Muslim women wearing a long modest dress and head covering (hijab). In the popular media we see fanatical terrorists and suicide bombers. But this is not what Islam is about.

The shell is the history and culture which gave birth to Islam and the institutions that developed as Islam grew to become a world religion. Islam was born in Arabia and reflects the culture of its origins. But Arab countries make up only a fraction of the Islamic world. Many customs associated with Arabs or Islam are rooted in a local culture rather than the actual teachings of Islam.

The nutmeat represents the practices and beliefs of Islam—the five pillars and beliefs discussed in Chapter 8.

The oil is the spiritual, innermost part of Islam. Oil makes a fine metaphor of the Spirit. Olive oil was used in the daily life for light and food. It was also used in the anointing of priests and kings.

The oil in the walnut nourishes the germ of life at the heart of the nut. Once the rest of the walnut has dissolved, this germ of life springs forth to produce a new living tree.

We cannot directly see the Spirit that is the source of eternal life. We only see the results of the Spirit in people's lives, and in the inspired scriptures, stories, poems, parables and songs which they have produced.

Islam has its parable of Muslim spirituality. The metaphor used is a Garden. Christians and Jews should easily recognize this metaphor, for it is derived from the Garden of Eden. Islam's metaphor can easily be applied to Christians and Jews, for it is part of our common story.

Let's explore this Garden from the Quran and the Bible.

THE GARDEN WITH RIVERS UNDERNEATH

*A **parable** of the Garden promised to the righteous is*

this: in it are rivers of water, of which the taste changes not, and rivers of milk, unchanging in taste, and rivers of wine, delicious to them who drink it, and rivers of pure honey. Therein they shall enjoy all kinds of fruits, and forgiveness from their Lord. (47: 15)

Note that this is a **parable**. The Garden represents the bliss of living in God's presence and favor. When we walk in the way of God, God plants this garden in our hearts. This is a hidden garden, below the level of our awareness.

As we read in both Genesis and the Quran, God brings us into life by breathing into us of his Spirit.

Then he made him complete and breathed into him of his Spirit and gave you seeing and hearing and hearts to under-stand—but little thanks to you give him. (Quran 32:8)

The Lord God formed the man from the dust of the earth and breathed into his nostrils the breath of life...Now the Lord God had planted a garden in the east. The Lord God took the man and put him in the garden to work it and take care of it. (Gen. 2: 7, 8,15).

God planted this garden; our job is to cultivate it and care for it. We cultivate this garden by responding to God's grace and doing the will of God. If we carefully cultivate it, this garden will produce delicious fruit on *"trees pleasing to the eye and good for food."* (Gen. 2:9).

If we neglect it, our garden will be overrun with wild brambles and noxious weeds—fuel for the fires of God's judgment. Meanwhile, we will find ourselves outside the garden, with the tree of life beyond our reach.

When we die, the husk of our organic life drops away, and the Garden of our heart is revealed. This Garden unfolds and becomes the new world in which we now live.

According to Islam, there is a further unfolding that takes place on the Day of Resurrection. This bliss is beyond anything we can know or imagine. *"And the greatest of all is God's good pleasure."* (9:72)

This Garden expands forever as we learn and grow throughout eternity with God.

> *But those who keep their duty to the Lord, for them are high places, about them are higher places built for them. (39:20)*

In the Quran, four rivers flow through this Garden. They consist of pure water, milk, wine, and honey. These are spiritual metaphors as well. Zafrulla Khan describes them as: (Khan 1970)

- **The pure water** represents all the blessings of God that sustain us in life.
- **The milk** is our experiencing the attributes of God who is most gracious, ever merciful, and compassionate to all.

- **The wine** represents the love of God. It is *"sparkling white, delicious, not intoxicating."*
- **Honey** represents being enfolded in the mercy and grace of God.

In Genesis, a single river flows through the Garden. But outside the garden the river divides and becomes four rivers. These are often understood as the four great rivers whose valleys are the birthplace of the great civilizations of the ancient world—the Nile, Euphrates, Tigris, and Hindi Rivers.

When we are in right relationship with God there is only the one River of Life. But outside of the Garden, the river is diverted to serve a divided world, with its rival empires and warring nations.

In the New Testament, the rivers represent the Holy Spirit flowing out from the life of the followers of Christ. As Jesus said and John explains:

> *If anyone is thirsty, let him come to me and drink. Whoever believes in me, as the Scripture has said, streams of living water will flow from within him. By this he meant the Spirit, whom those who believed in him were later to receive.* (John 7: 37-38)

This river metaphor is carried forward in the book of Revelation. In this vision, the Garden has become the City of God. The river of life flows from the throne of God and the Lamb. It produces a crop of fruit every month, and its leaves are the healing of the nations. (Rev.22: 1-2).

The apostle Paul describes the fruit of the Spirit as *"love, joy, peace, patience, kindness, goodness, gentleness, and self-control."* (Gal. 5:22)

This fruit of the Spirit is highly valued and sought after by many devout Muslims, Christians, and Jews.

Do all Muslims attain to this level of deep spirituality? Perhaps not. That may the case with many Christians and Jews as well.

But the yearning is there, whether it is recognized or not. As someone said, "There is a God-shaped hole in every heart, and we can never be complete and satisfied until it is filled by God."

The apostle Paul said it this way:

> *God did this so that men would seek him and perhaps reach out for him and find him, though he is not far from each one of us. For in Him we live and move and have our being.* (Acts 17: 27-28)

I know of some Muslims who have devoted their lives to filling that God-shaped hole in the heart. These are called "Sufis."

JESUS AND THE SUFI MYSTICS

The word "Sufi" means "of wool." Sufis are Muslim mystics who have "put on the wool," that is, they have adopted the rough robe of the poor and humble. Many of the Sufis are looked upon as saints, even though they often go beyond the conventions of traditional Islam.

Sufism is about loving God and being loved by God in a deeply personal way. And who better than Jesus can lead us into the very heart of God.

Sufi spirituality is expressed in stories, poetry, art, calligraphy, prayer, rituals, exercises and dances. From Sufi dances comes the expression "Whirling Dervishes."

These exercises are intended to induce a state of mystical union with God, often after a night of prayer, singing, and dancing.

My favorite Sufi poet is Jalahuddin Rumi, who lived in Turkey (1207-1273 AD). Rumi and other Sufi poets looked beneath the externals of religion to the Spirit at the heart of the believer. Rumi wrote:

> We (God) have placed in you a substance, a seeking, a yearning, and we are watching over it and won't let it be lost, but will bring it to its destined place.

> The seeds of His (God's) love blossom in every heart. The sounds of His flute fill every celebration. Everyone thinks that he sings and dances. But no—He (God) alone is the only one singing, He is the only one dancing." (Star 1997)

To some Sufis, Jesus was a role model and mentor, the embodiment of perfect love and submission. As Tarif

Khalidi wrote: "The Sufi mood began to treat Jesus as a figure of central spiritual relevance and affinity... The Jesus of Islamic Sufism became a figure not easily distinguished from the Jesus of the Gospels." (T. Khalidi, *The Muslim Jesus*, 2001)

I see the footsteps of Christ in this love and yearning of Sufis for union with God.

CHAPTER **12**

What We Learned

Harvie Conn observed that Muslims coming to Christ might be more of a "process of becoming" rather than a one-step decision. (Conn 1978)

A PROCESS OF BECOMING

Our Friendship Center experience confirmed this observation. Our Muslim friends told us, "You don't try to convert us. You just talk with us and slowly, slowly we are changed without knowing it."

The following chart illustrates what we observed in our Muslim friends over the years we were with them:

Response to the Gospel
-3   -2   -1   0   +1   +2   +3
Antagonistic   Indifferent   Receptive >>>> being "born of the Spirit >>>

These are only rough approximations. They are but milestones on a journey, not fixed positions. Each individual comes from a different starting point. People go forward and backward as they wrestle with issues of faith. They may be positive in one area and negative in another at the same time. Individual Muslims may be:

-3 **Very antagonistic** toward the Gospel. He may be a Muslim fundamentalist or extreme nationalist. He may identify Christianity with Western immorality and aggression (The Crusades, Christian Zionist support for Israel against Palestinians, etc).

-2 **Convinced Islam is superior** to Christianity. He wonders why Christians do not convert to Islam. However, he is not hostile to individual Christians.

-1 **Still convinced Islam is superior,** but is discovering that there are real Christian believers. He is taking fresh notice of Jesus as a prophet and messenger of God, and perhaps more.

-0 **Indifferent to the Gospel:** He may be a nominal Muslim, with little interest in religion. He may come to our Friendship Center to hang out for its social, educational, or recreational benefits. He is welcome, of course. We offered our friendship unconditionally.

+1 **Somewhat curious** about the Christian faith. He wants to know what we believe. He asks the usual questions about Jesus, the Bible, and how we regard Muhammad.

+ 2 **Desires a deeper understanding** of our Christian faith. He has begun to read the Bible and is asking searching questions. He may be aware on some level that his life is changing. He now understands that Christians do not believe in three gods.

+ 3 **A tentative follower of Jesus:** Jesus now occupies a meaningful place in his personal faith toward God. He may have had dreams about Jesus. He consciously thinks of Jesus in his prayers. He may have seen answers to prayer in Jesus' name.

He probably does not think of God as a Trinity. Such issues have become less important. What is important is having a personal relationship with God as a follower of Jesus.

These milestones are not static. What counts is not where you are on the chart. What matters is the direction you are moving. The person at -2 or -3 on the scale who is moving in the right direction may be closer to God than a person at + 3 who is moving in the wrong direction, or even standing still!

In making these assessments, we did not administer a questionnaire or formal interview. I made these rather subjective assessments based on our many hours of informal conversation. Genuine friendship and trust always took priority over scientific inquiry.

None of the Muslims who frequented our Center was very antagonistic toward Christians or the Christian faith. Most were at - 1 or - 2 on our scale at the beginning.

Virtually all of them moved a least a point or two in the positive direction. Some reached + 3 on our scale. A few went beyond the chart in their relationship with Christ.

Some may have become even better Muslims. After all, Islam is about submitting to God, and Jesus is a wonderful model of this submission.

BEING BORN OF THE SPIRIT

In my Christian upbringing, people talked about being "born again" as a one-time decision to "accept Christ as our Lord and Savior."

I have come to see that being "born of the Spirit" may be more of a lifelong process rather than a one-time decision. Looking back, I can see this was true in my own life, as well as for our Muslim friends.

I came forward in church and accepted Christ when I was seven years old. However, I had a relationship with Christ long before this time. In fact, I cannot remember a time when I did not know Jesus as my Savior.

For me, being "born of the Spirit" has been a lifelong process. Some areas of my life may still need spiritual rebirth. Even while we are dying, we are being "born from above."

Spiritual rebirth can be a rather mysterious process. As Jesus explained to Rabbi Nicodemus:

Spirit gives birth to spirit...The wind blows wherever it pleases. You hear the sound, but you cannot tell where it comes from, or where it is going. So it is with everyone born of the Spirit. (John 3: 6, 8)

In our Western culture, we put a high value on decisiveness and commitment. Sales managers train their sales people to "close the sale" and get the customer to "sign on the dotted line."

This carries over to how evangelists do their work. The evangelist pleads: "Make your decision for Christ today. Tomorrow may be too late. Make your salvation sure!"

This is our Western culture speaking. It does not carry over well into the Arab world.

"Inshallah" is an Arabic saying meaning, "As God wills." Arab culture tends to be more tentative than Western culture. In Islam, every human intention is subject to the will of God. ("Inshallah" is discussed in chapter 7, under the heading "Predestination.")

The Muslim who is moving toward Jesus must not be pushed into making a hasty decision or commitment. His approach to Christ is likely to be much more tentative. As one of our Muslim friends told us, "Slowly, slowly we are changed without knowing it."

Assurance of salvation: As a Christian, I have confidence in Christ's salvation from such scriptures as:

> *That if you confess with your mouth 'Jesus is Lord' and believe in your heart that God raised him from the dead, you will be saved.* (Rom. 10:9)
>
> *Whosoever believes and is baptized shall be saved.* (Mark 16:16)

The tentative Muslim follower of Jesus may not have the same confidence. But Muslims do not expect to know their eternal fate until the Day of Judgment. They take comfort in knowing that God is *"most compassionate, ever merciful, and most forgiving,"* as Islam teaches.

With all of our Christian confidence, we should not forget that we too are subject to God's discerning judgment: (Rom. 14:10)

> *For we must all appear before the judgment seat of Christ,*

that each one may receive what is due him for the things done while in the body, whether good or bad..the fire will test the quality of every man's work." (2 Cor. 5:10, 13)

SIGNS OF FAITH

Muslim followers of Jesus may be cautious about discussing their personal faith in Christ. Some Christians are like that as well. They simply may lack confidence. Perhaps their faith is obscured by doubts or perplexing questions.

God, however, looks deep into the human heart. If faith is there, God will find it, for He put it there in the first place. Faith comes to us as a work of God's grace.

Jesus was able to find faith in some unlikely candidates. He found faith in a Samaritan woman thirsty for "living water;" a Roman centurion concerned about his sick servant; and a Canaanite woman willing to be called a "dog" for the sake of her sick daughter. (John 4; Matt. 8, 15)

These people were neither Christians nor Jews. Jesus never asked them to convert to a different religion. Yet Jesus said of them, *"I tell you the truth, I have not found anyone in Israel with such great faith."* (Matt. 8: 10)

Faith does produce some outward signs. As Jesus said, *"By their fruit you shall know them."* Jesus refers to two such signs:

He who receives you: When Jesus sent out his disciples he told them: *"He who receives you receives me, and he who receives me receives him who sent me."* (Matt. 10:40).

We have been in scores of Muslim homes. Every family received us graciously. Much of this warmth was cultural. Hospitality is a prime Arab value. However, they knew we were Christians, and they received us in full knowledge and respect for our Christian faith. In so doing, these Muslim families were showing their respect for the One who sent us.

Our Muslim friends had enough faith to ask for our prayers. They prayed for us as well. Together, we learned what Peter discovered at the house of Cornelius: *"Now I realize that God does not show favoritism, but accepts men from every nation who fear him and do what is right."* (Acts. 10:34)

Sheep and goats: The parable of the sheep and goats on the Day of Judgment (Matt. 25) gives us another glimpse into how God reckons faith.

In this parable, God accepted the "sheep" because they had visited the sick and the prisoners and cared for the naked, hungry, and lonely. He excluded the "goats" because they failed to do the same.

This parable is full of surprises. The first surprise is that God is often present where we least expect Him. He was present in the prisons and among the poor and the suffering. The sheep and goats were both surprised to learn this.

The sheep were surprised to discover that they were

sheep. They were not necessarily religious. They were just doing what they thought was right. But God saw in them a faith which they themselves did not see.

The goats were surprised to learn that they were goats. They believed all the right doctrines and said the right words. They were surprised at how little this counted in God's judgment. They were shocked to find themselves "in the dark."

We Christians have a surprise for us. We Christians may think we know who is "in" and who is "out." But not so in this parable. It was not until the Day of Judgment that we discover who are the "sheep" and who are the "goats."

I believe these parables may apply to our Muslim followers of Jesus as well as to us.

THE BARE NECESSITIES

I posed the question earlier: "What minimum theological understanding would be required of a Muslim follower of Jesus who remains a Muslim? What Christian doctrines and practices would such a follower need to embrace? What of Islam would the Muslim follower of Jesus need to leave behind?

Remember, the Muslim follower of Jesus is not converting to Christianity. No one is examining him for baptism or church membership. He is just trying to follow Jesus, as a good Muslim should.

His understanding of Jesus will likely be a mixture of what he reads in the New Testament, and in the Quran.

His beginning point will be the high regard and respect that Islam gives to Jesus as the Messiah and the Word of God. How far he or she goes beyond this will depend on God's grace and guidance. We could only take our Muslim friends as far as God leads them, and they were willing to follow. That is true for us as well.

The early believers: The first believers in Jesus were Jews, not Christians. Their scriptures were the Old Testament. As James told Paul, *"You see brother, how many thousands of Jews have believed, and all of them are zealous for the Law."* (Acts 21: 20)

These early disciples were saved without any knowledge of the Trinity or the dual nature of Christ. Their only scripture was the Old Testament.

They were justified by faith. They trusted in God according to the grace they had received. This is true for us as well, and for Muslims who will follow Jesus according to the grace and light they have received.

Practicing Islam as a follower of Jesus: The Muslim would be free to observe the "Five Pillars" of Islam. Prayer, fasting, and giving alms to the poor are commendable practices whether one is a Christian or a Muslim. Whether he makes a pilgrimage to Mecca will be a matter of personal choice.

If he comes to believe in Jesus' death on the cross, other Muslims might consider him mildly heretical in this belief. However, God's forgiveness does not depend on everyone having the correct doctrine of atonement.

God's forgiveness stems from God's faithful love and concern for our well-being. For a Christian, God has revealed this love in Christ's death on the cross. God has revealed His power in raising Christ from the dead.

Christians and Muslims might both regard the Muslim follower of Jesus as mildly heretical. But God knows the heart, and that is what really counts.

NINETEEN YEARS LATER

We lost contact with most of our Muslim friends as soon as we returned to the U.S. These were the days before internet and e-mail. Few of the Palestinian villagers had access to telephone service at that time.

One of our friends did immigrate to the U.S. and is now living in Washington State. He has made several trips back to Bethlehem to visit his family there.

One of our American student interns returned to Israel-Palestine after graduating from college. He and his wife started a new Friendship Center in Ramallah.

Just recently, a few of our Muslim friends have discovered my web site, davidteeter.org. They have since contacted us by e-mail and phone. Two of our Muslim friends came through Tacoma on speaking tours, and we were able to meet them briefly.

Of course, they are now married, middle-aged, with teen-aged children. Several have established their own centers in the Bethlehem area. These are not exact replicas of our Friendship Center. Each new center reflects the talents, interests, and vision of its founder. One center has its focus in the arts. Another has its focus on peace and reconciliation. Another provides health services in a rural village.

We have seen the truth of Jesus' saying:

Unless a kernel of wheat falls into the ground and dies, it remains only a single seed. But if it dies, it produces many seeds." (John 12: 23).

We had to die to our vision of a "Muslim Followers of Jesus" movement. That death did not come easily or quickly. Now, years later, some of the seed we planted is springing up with new life.

CONCLUSIONS AND QUESTIONS

When it comes to reaching Muslims for Christ, there is no substitute for love. No amount of clever argument will work if the love is not there. If Muslims are to receive our witness, we must be prepared to hear them as well.

The most difficult issue was how Muslim followers of

Jesus will find spiritual nurture, fellowship, and worship with others of like faith. We were not able to take them this far before our time ran out. Leaving them when we did broke our hearts.

Implications for Muslim evangelism: Conventional, Western-style evangelism has made hardly any inroads in the Muslim world, and it probably never will. Muslim evangelism struggles against a heavy burden of history. Muslims have long been exposed to the dark side of a loveless Christianity. This is not just ancient history, either.

Christianity has its modern day crusaders, who promote the idea of a clash of civilizations, who see every Muslim or Arab as a terrorist enemy, and who would push the world toward a bloody Armageddon.

In Israel, thousands of foreign Christians march noisily through the streets of Jerusalem every year, proclaiming their support for Israel's government, and urging Israel to seize more land without regard to its Palestinian inhabitants.

This history makes it much more difficult for Muslim people to see the love of Christ in the Christian religion. Without this love, Christianity is but a noisy gong and a clanging cymbal.

We have seen that genuine, unconditional love can overcome this dark burden of history. Muslim hearts will open to people who live Christ's love in their midst.

Meanwhile, God may have some undisclosed purpose

for keeping Christianity, Judaism, and Islam as separate and distinct religions. Perhaps each of these religions contains something of value that would be lost if merged into one super-religion. In the words of Isaiah:

> *As when juice is found in a cluster of grapes and men say, "don't destroy it, there is yet some good in it." So will I do on behalf of my servants; I will not destroy them all.* (Isa. 65: 8)

We can apply this verse to Israel and Palestine. Both are worth saving. Both have something to contribute to the family of nations. Like all nations, each has its dark side. Still, I have hope that the better impulses I have known and witnessed in both peoples will prevail in the end. For scripture tells us:

> *That at the name of Jesus every knee should bow, in heaven and earth and under the earth, and every tongue confess that Jesus Christ is Lord to the glory of God the Father.* (Phil. 2:10)

I do not yet understand how this will come about. I do not think everyone in the world will convert to Christianity. Christianity itself has its dark side that needs to be conformed to Christ. Meanwhile, I left pondering two questions:

1. Is it possible that some people are following Christ, without being fully aware of whom they are following?

2. Is it possible that Christ is speaking to some people, but in a metaphor and language that we do not recognize as "Christian"?

How this has affected my own Christian faith. I am a lifelong Christian through and through. I found it very enlightening to look at my faith through the eyes of people with a different worldview. In our conversations with Muslims, we faced questions we would never otherwise consider. These experiences have greatly enriched my Christian faith.

Just maybe, some who read this story will also hear the call of Christ and follow His footsteps into the very hearts of Muslim people.

Part 3
Sharing the Land of Promise

For I know the plans I have for you, declares the Lord, plans to prosper you and not to harm you, plans to give you a hope and a future. (Jer. 29:11)

Whereby Allah guides him who seeks His good pleasure unto the paths of peace, and brings them forth from the shadows into the light by his will. He guides them into the straight path. (Quran 5:16)

He (Jesus) came and preached peace to you who were far away and peace to those who were near. (Eph. 2: 17)

The Old City in Jerusalem

CHAPTER **13**

The Rocky Road to Peace

People often tell me, "Jews and Arabs have been fighting for thousands of years. They will never make peace."

That is simply not true. Jews and Arabs have lived peacefully together for centuries in Palestine under various rulers. The current conflict began with the birth of the Jewish Zionist movement at the end of the 19th century.

People often ask, "Is there any hope for Middle East peace?" My answer is yes, I have hope. Hope, however, is not quite the same thing as optimism.

Optimism may be nothing more than wishful thinking. Some people are naturally optimistic, a matter of good brain chemistry.

Hope goes deeper than optimism. My hope is anchored in my faith in God, and in God's purpose for humanity.

Polls taken in Israel and Palestine have consistantly shown that a majority of people on both sides want peace and would accept two States—Israel and Palestine—living side by side in peace. But a majority on both sides now doubt that their respective governments will be able to solve the problems involved.

The heavier burden: Here in Part 3, the focus shifts to Israel. We spent a lot of time in Israel even while we were working with Palestinians in Bethlehem. We had many Israeli friends. We want God's shalom for Israelis as well as for the Palestinians.

As I see it, Israel must carry the heavier burden of peace making. There is a huge power imbalance in Israel's favor.

Israel has all the instruments of statehood, the most powerful military in the region, and the lion's share of the land. *"To whom much is given, much is required."*

Israel exercises military and economic control over the territories. Palestinians can do little without Israel's consent, or at least non-interference. A weak Palestinian leadership is split between the more moderate Fatah party, and Hamas, the hard line Islamic fundamentalist party. Hamas has been gaining influence due to the inability of the moderates to make any progress with ending the Israeli occupation.

Some Palestinians have tried to offset Israel's power advantage by resorting to terrorism. That has only served to stiffen Israel's resolve and tighten its control over the Palestinian territories.

Israel's number one concern is security, and that is a

legitimate concern. However, Security will only come by resolving the conflict. In Hebrew, security is an attribute of shalom/peace. Security cannot be a **pre-requisite** for progress in peace making.

The violent elements in Palestinian society get their influence from anger and hopelessness. Only a renewal of hope can silence those voices. In building that hope, Israel can be either part of the problem, or part of the solution. Meanwhile, Israel has its own dilemma, springing from the very roots of Zionism.

ISRAEL'S DILEMMA

Israel's dilemma stems from the conflicting goals of Zionism. The early Zionists set forth three objectives for a Jewish State in Palestine.

- A Jewish State for the Jewish people.
- A democratic government.
- The ancient Land of Israel.

Zionism began with the slogan, "A land without a people for a people without a land."

But Palestine was hardly "a land without a people." It was a settled land of villages, towns, and cities. A 1922 census found a population of 668,258 Arabs and 83,780 Jews. (Epp 1970)

Israel's first Prime Minister, David Ben Gurion acknowledged:

Jewish villages were built in the place of Arab villages. You do not even know the names of these Arab villages, and I do not blame you because geography books no longer exist. Not only do the books not exist, the Arab villages are not there either... There is not a single place built in this country that did not have a former Arab population. (Goldmann 1978)

Arabs were still in the majority in 1947. That was the dilemma facing the Jewish community in 1947. With an Arab majority, the new Jewish state could not be both Jewish **and** democratic!

The United Nations came up with what seemed to be the only feasible solution that would work for both peoples.

The U.N. Partitioning Plan: In 1947, the U.N. proposed dividing Palestine between a Jewish state and an Arab state. The Jewish state would receive about 55 percent of the land. The Arab state would receive the remaining 45 percent.

The Zionist movement was deeply divided over this plan. The mainstream Zionists saw this plan as a solution to the demographic problem. Israel would be smaller, but Jewish and democratic. David Ben Gurion's mainstream party accepted the U.N. Partition Plan.

The opposing Zionists were known as the Revisionists.

Ze'ev Jabotinsky (1880-1940) was the founder of this movement. He believed that the Jewish State should never give up any part of the "Promised Land." In fact, he and his followers wanted the Jewish State to include land on both sides of the Jordan River.

He believed that the Arab people would never accept a Jewish state in Palestine. Israel's only hope was to build an "iron wall" of invincible military might. This "iron wall" doctrine still influences Israel's defense and foreign policies.

The Revisionists rejected the U.N. Partition Plan. They formed their own military units. One of the units was known as the Irgun. Menachim Begin was one of its leaders. Yitzhaq Shamir led a smaller group split off from the Irgun. This group was called the Stern Gang, or Lehi.

Both of these groups carried out terrorist campaigns against the British and the Arabs. Begin's Irgun blew up the King David Hotel in Jerusalem in 1946, killing 91 people, including some Jews. I mentioned in Part 1 that a sister of our three landladies was killed in that explosion.

Begin's Irgun also carried out the massacre of the Arab village of Deir Yassin, on April 4, 1948. More than a hundred Arab villagers were killed, including women and children. This was just before the start of the 1948 War of Independence.

The U.N. sent Count Bernadotte of Sweden to mediate the conflict between the Jews and the Arabs. He was assassinated by Shamir's Stern Gang. (Schlaim 2001)

The mainstream Zionists and the Revisionists went to the brink of civil war over the U.N. Partition Plan. But Begin realized that Jews fighting Jews would only concede the outcome to the Palestinians.

He and the other Revisionists agreed to let David Ben Gurion lead as Prime Minister of the new State of Israel. The Revisionists formed an opposition party, called the Herud. The Herud later became the Likud party. This party and its more extreme allies are known as the "Greater Israel" movement.

Both Menachim Begin and Yitzhak Shamir later served as Prime Ministers in Israel. Ironically, it was Menachim Begin who signed the peace treaty in 1979 giving the Sinai back to Egypt.

The Palestinian Arabs rejected the U.N. Partitioning Plan. They saw that the Jews, with their smaller population, were getting 55 percent of the land. The Arabs, with their larger population, were left with only 45 percent. (A real bargain for the Arabs, given what transpired. Today they are hard pressed to hold on to just 22 percent of the land. And much of that 22 percent is taken up by Jewish settlements.)

The U.N. plan died stillborn. In 1948, Israel declared itself an independent State. The surrounding Arab states declared war against the new State of Israel.

The 1948 War: The 1948 War brought victory for Israel. But for the Palestinians it was a catastrophe. Thousands of Arabs fled or were driven out of Israel.

Most ended up in refugee camps in the West Bank territories and neighboring Arab countries.

The Israeli government insists that the Arabs left voluntarily. The Palestinians insist they were driven out by force. Israel's "new historians" tend to support the Palestinian claim. For more information I recommend:

- *The Iron Wall*, by Avi Shlaim. (Schlaim 2001)
- *Scars of War, Wounds of Peace*, by Shlomo Ben-Ami. (Ben-Ami 2006)
- *The Birth of the Palestinian Refugee Problem*, by Benny Morris. (Morris 1988)

For a Palestinian perspective, I suggest two books by Christian Palestinians whose families were caught up in the events of the Palestinian tragedy:

- *Through the Eyes of the Victims*, by Alex Awad. (Awad 2001)
- *Blood Brothers*, by Elias Chacour. (Chacour 2003)

In any event, Israel ended up with 78 percent of historic Palestine. The Palestinians were left with the remaining 22 percent. Nor did the Palestinians have much contol of their 22 percent. The West Bank remained under Jordanian rule; the Gaza Strip under Egyptian rule.

After the war, Arabs remaining within Israel made up only 20 percent of Israel's population. This minority no longer posed an obstacle to the Jewish character of the State of Israel. They were granted Israeli citizenship.

The following map roughly illustrates the 1949 division between Israel and the Palestinian territories.

The 1967 Six Day War: Israel captured the West Bank from the Jordanians, and the Gaza Strip from the Egyptians. Once again Israel was faced with the Jewish-Democracy-Land dilemma: What to do with the millions of Arabs, many of them refugees, who lived in the territories now occupied by Israel?

If these territories were incorporated into Israel, the Palestinians would soon become a majority in the larger Israel. Israel would lose either its Jewish character or its democracy.

Israel decided not to incorporate these territories into the State of Israel. Instead, the territories remained under Israeli military occupation. The Palestinians were left in political limbo.

The Israeli government has long tried to dismiss the very existence of the Palestinians as a people. Prime Minister Golda Meir once declared, "There is no such thing as a Palestinian people... It is not as if we came and threw them out and took their country. They didn't exist." (Meir 1969)

The 1949 armistace boundary between Israel and the West Bank territory was originally marked on maps by a green line. The Israeli government has since removed the green line from their maps and renamed the West Bank "Judea and Samaria."

But none of these fictions have solved Israel's dilemma. The Palestinians are still there, and they have not given up their national aspirations.

The 1993 Oslo Accord awakened new hopes for peace. The PLO recognized the State of Israel. Israel began negotiating with the PLO toward a Palestinian State. But two shocking events shattered these hopes.

On March 7, 1994, an armed Jewish settler name Baruch Goldstein entered the Mosque of Abraham in Hebron. He opened fire on the Muslims at prayer, killing 29 and wounding 150. He was finally subdued and beaten to death by the survivors. His grave has since become a pilgrimage shrine for Israeli extremists.

On November 4, 1995, a Jewish extremist shot and killed Prime Minister Yitzhaq Rabin. His assassination stunned the nation. Ironically, the Israelis elected a new right wing government, led by Benjamin Netanyahu, who opposed the Oslo Accord signed by Yitzhaq Rabin.

Netanyahu was a "Greater Israel" advocate and a strong supporter of Jewish settlements. He declined to follow through with Israel's Oslo commitments.

The Second Intifada: The failure of the 2000 Camp David summit led to a second Intifada (Palestinian uprising). The trigger was Ariel Sharon's provocative trespass of Muslim holy sites on the Temple Mount.

The more extreme groups of Palestinians adopted a new and dreadful terror tactic—suicide bombings. Extremists in Gaza also began launching primitive rockets at nearby Israeli towns.

Israel responded by sealing Gaza off from Israel and

the rest of the world. Gaza became a virtual prison. In 2008, a massive Israeli military invasion further devastated Gaza. There were hundreds of civilian casualties.

The Israelis are building a "separation wall" down the length of the West Bank. Travel and commerce between Palestinian towns and villages are cut off by numerous Israeli check points. Israeli settlement expansion is still taking place.

As of this writing, Israel has a new government led once more by Benjamin Netanyahu of the Likud party. He is under pressure from his more extreme coalition partners on one hand, and the U.S. administration of President Obama on the other hand.

In short, there have been many moves towards peace since we left Israel in 1989, and many setbacks. I am still hopeful, but not yet optimistic.

ISRAEL'S GOVERNMENT

Unlike America's "winner take all" two party system, Israel has a parliamentary system. Every ethnic, religious, and ideologic faction in Israel has its own political party. Each of these parties has its own agenda.

No one party in Israel has ever won a majority of seats in the Knesset. To form a government, the new prime minister must put together a coalition with a number of smaller parties. To get their support, the prime minister must give each coalition partner one or more ministries in his cabinet.

The result is huge, unwieldly cabinets. Since cabinet ministers represent different parties, their agendas often conflict with that of the prime minister.

Prime ministers in Israel are not the strong chief executives as are American presidents. Most decisions require a majority vote of the cabinet members.

Any movement toward peace brings threats from some of these smaller parties to pull out of the coalition and bring down the government. This applies to any efforts to rein in the Jewish settlers in the territories.

Jewish Settlements: These enclaves within the Palestinian territories are not small clusters of make-shift huts. They are self-contained towns and small cities, with up to 35,000 residents. Many have parks, schools, their own police departments. There is even a university. Some 300,000 settlers live in 120 or more settlements. The settlements are connected to Israel and to one another by Jewish-only roads.

While the built up towns cover only 2% of the West Bank, the settlements control 40% of the land through access roads and expansive municipal boundaries.

These settlements not only take up a lot of Palestinian land and water resources, they also carve up the Palestinian territories into disconnected enclaves.

In addition to these "authorized" settlements, there is another 100 or more "illegal" outposts, mostly consisting of trailers and other portable structures.

Occasionally, by order of the Israeli High Court, the

army will tear down one or two of the "illegal" outposts. This usually provokes riots by the settlers, who usually return a few days later to replace the buildings and reoccupy the outpost.

Israel's Chief Justice of the High Court Dorit Breinisch recently complained about these illegal (under Israeli law) outposts. He told the defense minister:

"For years, we have been hearing from you about demolition orders that the authorities issue. But each time, nothing happens."

The U.N. Security Council and other international bodies regard all Jewish settlements in the occupied territories to be illegal.

There are powerful Israeli political interests behind the ever expanding settlements. Their strategy is to make it politically impossible for Israel to give up the land required for a viable Palestinian state. They call it "making facts on the ground."

Regardless of which party is in office, settlement expansion has continued unabated.

An Israeli watchdog group, *Peace Now*, keeps track of settlement activities. Their web site provides maps and statistics of Jewish settlement activities.

The Israeli government can be very decisive when it comes to making war. But peace making with the Palestinians has led only to paralysis, and eventually, collapse of the governing coalition.

The Monkey and the Banana: You may have heard the story of the monkey and the banana in a narrow necked jar. The monkey spies the banana in the jar. He reaches in to grasp the banana. But with his fist clenched around the banana, he cannot withdraw his hand. He won't let go of the banana. So he is stuck with his hand in the jar.

The Palestian territories have become the banana in the monkey story. The Palestinian's high birth rate is the jar.

That is Israel's unresolved dilemna: If Israel is to retain its Jewish character and remain a democracy, it will have to relinquish the Palestinian territories. If instead Israel annexes the territories, it loses either its Jewish character, or its democracy.

To date, no Israeli government has been able to resolve this dilemma. Meanwhile, the Palestinians remain in limbo under Israeli military occupation.

Yet I have hope. In the remaining chapters I will lay out the reason for this hope.

CHAPTER 14

A Parable of a Missed Opportunity

I've often been asked: "How can you reconcile the harsh, warlike, tribal God of the Old Testament with Jesus' teachings of a God whose redemptive love embraces the whole world?" The scriptures give us a progressive revelation of God. Some passages reflect Israel's origins as a collection of tribes coming out of slavery in Egpyt. They were fighting for survival against fierce rivals already settled in the land.

These ancient Israelites needed a fierce tribal God who could defeat the gods of their enemies. In this view, Israel's God was for Israel only.

The Hebrew prophets offer a more universal vision of Israel, and Israel's God. In this vision, God called Israel to be a *"light to the nations."* Israel's God is a God for all nations.

It was not God who changed over the centuries. It was the people and their circumstances that had changed.

THE PROPHETIC VISION

This new insight shed a different light on God's promise to Abraham. In Genesis, God tells Abraham:
> *You will be the father of many nations... and all the peoples of the earth will be blessed by you."* (Gen. 12: 2,3).

The prophets had a vision of how this blessing could be realized. Isaiah and Micah proclaimed:
> *Many peoples will come and say,"Come, let us go up to the mountain of the Lord, to the house of the God of Jacob. He will teach us his ways, so that we may walk in his paths."* (Isa. 2:2,3)

> *Let no foreigner who has bound himself to the Lord say, the Lord will surely exclude me from his people.* (Isa.56:3)

> *For my house will be called a house of prayer for all nations.* (Isa. 56:7)

> *Nations will come to your light, and kings to the brightness of your dawn.* (Isa. 60:3).

Jews returning from the Babylonian exile would not be returning to an empty land. If they were to be a *"light to the nations,"* they would have to share the land with its non-Jewish inhabitants.

Ezekiel gave the returning Jews a new set of instructions regarding these non-Jewish inhabitants.

> *You are to distribute this land among yourselves according to the tribes of Israel. You are to allot it as an inheritance for yourselves and for the aliens who have settled among you and who have children.*

> *You are to consider them as native-born Israelites; along with you they are to be allotted an inheritance among the tribes of Israel. In whatever tribe the alien settles, there you are to give him his inheritance, declares the Sovereign Lord.* (Ezek. 47:21-23)

But the returning Jews did not all share this prophetic vision of God for all nations. For them, Israel's God was still a God for Israel only.

THE MAKING OF AN ENEMY

In 538 BC, Jews were given permission to return to Judea to rebuild the temple in Jerusalem.

Some 50,000 Jews returned to Judea in the first wave of returnees. Among them were more than 5000 priests, levites, singers, and other temple functionaries. They were all eager to rebuild the temple and reestablish priestly worship in Jerusalem. An altar was built and the foundations of the temple were laid.

The Samaritans from northern Israel learned of the

new temple being built in Jerusalem. They approached the Jewish leadership with an offer to help:

> *Let us help you build because, like you, we seek your God and have been sacrificing to him since the time of Esarhaddon king of Assyria, who brought us here.* (Ezra 4: 2).

Here was a golden opportunity to realize Isaiah's vision of Zion as a *"light to the nations,"* with the Lord's house *"a house of prayer for all nations."*

But the Jews were most concerned about preserving the purity of the Jewish people and religion. They rudely rejected the Samaritan's offer. *"You have no part with us in building a temple to our God."*

The disappointed Samaritans complained to the Persian officials. The Persian officials issued a stop work order on the temple construction. The work remained halted for 17 long years.

The temple was eventually rebuilt, but it was not to be a *"house of prayer for all nations."* It was a Jewish temple for a Jewish only God.

Ezra's Arrival. Ezra the priest arrived in Jerusalem around 440 BC." He was shocked to discover that many of the Jewish men had married non-Jewish women. He set up a divorce court and demanded that all Jewish men divorce their non-Jewish wives. Ezra, like the earlier Jewish returnees, was not prepared to share his religion with non-Jews.

Led by Nehemiah, the Jews built a fortified wall around Jerusalem as a defence against their enemies—enemies created by their own fear and hatred of "the other."

They found justification for these actions in Ezra's new edition of the "Book of the Law":

> *The Book of Moses was read aloud in the hearing of the people and there it was found that no Ammonite or Moabite should ever be admitted into the assembly of God...When the people heard this, they excluded* **from Israel all who were of foreign descent.** (Neh. 13:3, quoting Deut. 23:3)

The Jewish returnees had misidentified the people of the land. They regarded the Samaritans as if they were the Canaanites of old. They remembered how the early Canaanites had seduced the Israelites into idolatry. But the Samaritans were not the same people as the ancient Canaanites (nor are the Palestinians of today).

CANAANITES, SAMARITANS, AND PALESTINIANS.

The Canaanites. The "Canaanites" of Abraham's day were mostly Amorites, Hittites, and Hurrians. Amorite means "Western Semite." Abraham himself was of "Western Semite" stock.

In Abraham's day, the Amorites knew and respected the God of Abraham. There were righteous kings among them. Genesis gives examples in Melchizedek (Gen. 13) and Abimelech. Abraham and Isaac lived peaceably among them, trading and making treaties with them. (Gen.20, 26)

God told Abraham that his descendants must remain in Egypt for 400 years before they could return to possess the land of promise. *"For the sins of the Amorites have not yet reached its full measure."* (Gen. 15: 13,16).

Over the next several centuries, the Amorites would adopt the most debased practices of Canaanite idolary, such as shrine prostitution and the sacrifice of infants. But in the days of Abraham, Isaac, and Jacob they had not yet reached the tipping point in this decline.

When the Israelites finally returned from Egypt, they brought God's judgment against a culture that had debased itself beyond recovery.

Moses told the Israelites they were to *"destroy totally"* the seven nations that made up the Canaanites of that period. *"Make no treaty and show them no mercy."* (Deut.7:2)

The ancient Moabites were a different story. They were excluded from Israel because they had denied the tribes of Israel safe passage during their journey to the promised land.

(The book of Ruth may have been written as a prophetic protest against the anti-foreign fears of the Jews of Ezra's company. For King David himself (and Jesus) are descendents of Ruth the Moabite.)

The Samaritans. The Samaritans of Ezra's day were not the Canaanites of Joshua's time. Nor were they the Moabites of Moses' time. The Samaritans origin is explained in 2 Kings 17.

In 721 BC, the Assyrians conquered Israel and took all but a remnant into exile. Conquered peoples from other regions were transplanted into the land of Israel in their place.

The Assyrian rulers sent Israelite priests back to Israel to teach these new residents to worship the God of Israel. It was an imperfect conversion, however, as some of the new converts retained their old household gods (as did Jacob's wives).

The remaining Israelites intermarried with these foreign converts. Their descendants became the Samaritan people. These were the people that Ezra despised and rejected as "foreigners."

The Samaritans came seeking to learn more and to worship the God of Israel at the new temple.

In rejecting the Samaritans, the Jews of Ezra's time were rejecting the prophetic vision of Israel as a "light to the nations." The result was, they turned potential co-worshippers into bitter and disillusioned enemies.

The breach between the Samaritans and Jews was never healed. The Samaritans build their own temple on Mt. Gerazim, near the town of Shechem (now Nablis). Around 125 BC, a Jewish army led by the High Priest destroyed the Samaritan temple.

There are some 400 Samaritans living in Palestine today, in the Nablus vicinity. Each year, they sacrifice a sheep to celebrate Passover on top of Mt. Gerazim.

The Palestinians. The Palestinians of today are **not** the idolatrous Canaanites of Joshua's day. They are a mixture of all the peoples who have lived in the land from the beginning of time. Some are descended from Jews who converted to Christianity or Islam. Others arrived from Arabia when the Muslims captured Jerusalem in 637 AD.

Some are Christians; most are Muslims. All worship the God of Abraham, Isaac, and Jacob.

A CHOICE OF VISIONS AND VOICES

History is being made today by Israelis and Palestinians. Partisans on all sides can find in scripture justification for the path they take. There are many voices proclaiming "this is the way." The outcome will depend on which voice is ultimately heard.

- Moses said: *"Destroy them totally. Make no treaties; show no mercy."* (Deut. 7:2)
- Nehemiah said: *"Expel the foreigners."* (Neh. 13:3)
- Ezekiel said, *"Consider the foreigner the same as an Israelite."* (Eze.47:23)
- Moses also said, *"Love the foreigner as yourselves."* (Lev. 19:35).
- Jesus said, *"Love your enemies."* (Matt. 5: 44).

Muslims can find in their Holy Quran words that lead to lasting peace, and words that lead to perpetual war. We all need to make sure we are hearing the right voices.

It is Ezekiel's voice that needs to be heard today, not Joshua's. We who are Christians should be listening to Jesus, who said "love your enemies," not Nehemiah, who said "exclude them from Israel."

But is there **biblical** hope for Jews and Arabs sharing the land promised to Abraham and his descendants? I believe so. That is the topic of the next chapter.

CHAPTER 15

A Biblical Case for Sharing the Land

The Hebrew scriptures call it the "Land of Canaan." The Romans renamed it "Palestine." Israelis call it "The Land of Israel."

Today this land is home to some 5 million Jews and 4.5 million Palestinian Arabs. Millions more Jews, Christians, and Muslims have deep spiritual, historical, and emotional ties to the land.

History has led to this reality: Neither side can realize its national hopes without recognizing the needs of the other. Israelis and Palestinians are stuck with each other. The two sides must find some way of sharing the land that will meet the needs of both peoples.

In this chapter we explore some **biblical** considerations about sharing the Land of Promise. We will look for answers for three questions:

1. To whom was the land promised?

2. What are the obligations that go with the land?
3. What about the native non-Jewish people of the land?

THE PROMISE

At God's command, Abraham set out on a journey to the Land of Canaan. Upon Abraham's arrival in the land, God told him:

To your offspring I will give this land. (Gen. 12:7)

Lift up your eyes from where you are and look north and south, east and west. All the land that you see I will give to you and your offspring forever... Go, walk through the length and breadth of the land for I am giving it to you. (Gen.13:14, 17)

To your descendants I give this land, from the the river of Egypt to the great river, the Euphrates. (Gen. 15: 18)

The whole land of Canaan, where you are now an alien, I will give as an everlasting possession to you and your descendants after you, and I will be your God. (Gen.17:8).

The Promise was about more than just real estate. For God had a greater purpose in calling Abraham. He told Abraham:

*I will make your name great, and you will be a blessing...
and all peoples on earth will be blessed for you.* (Gen. 12:
2,3)

A rabbi once explained to me: "God did not choose
the Jews for any special privilege. He called them for a special purpose. That purpose was to be a *light to the nations.*"

The Promised Land must be seen in the light of God's
higher purpose. God blessed Abraham so that Abraham
could become a blessing. God's intention is that all nations would be blessed in Father Abraham. That includes
the Palestinians.

The Promise is not about political states or national
sovereignty. God did not promise the land to the 21st
century State of Israel. The promise is about people—
Abraham's descendants.

This brings us to the question: "Who are Abraham's
descendants?

Abraham's Descendants: The Lord said concerning
Abraham:

> *For I have chosen him so that he will direct his children
> and his household after him to* **keep the way of the
> Lord by doing what is right and just,** *so the Lord
> will bring about for Abraham what he has promised him.*
> (Gen.18:19).

God's promise to Abraham does not happen automatically. In order for Abraham's promise to be realized, Abraham's children must *"keep the way of the Lord by doing what is right and just."*

The Promise was reaffirmed to Isaac and Jacob. But the young Jacob did not *"keep the way of the Lord."* Nor did he do *"what is right and just."*

Jacob swindled his brother Esau out of his birthright. He stole his father's blessing by deceit. Because of this, he was forced to flee from the land. For 20 years he lived as an exile in Syria. God allowed Jacob to return to the land only after Jacob's conversion from "Jacob" to "Israel."

Children by faith: Both Old and New Testaments affirm that the Promise is not based solely on physical descent. It is based on **active faith**. The apostle Paul wrote:

> *Therefore the Promise comes by faith, so that it may be guaranteed to all Abraham's offspring—not only to those who are of the Law, but also to those who are of the faith of Abraham. He is the father of us all. As it is written, "I have made you a father of many nations."*

We are neither qualified, nor disqualified from the Promise by our biological descent. The Promise is to those who by faith *"keep the way of the Lord and do what is right and just."*

Abraham's non-Jewish children: There were other children of Abraham who were not counted in the line of Jacob. They were children of Ishmael, Esau, and Abraham's third wife Keturah. But their faith found them a place in the Promise.

According to Judges and Chronicles, the territory of Judah was settled jointly by Jewish and Edomite clans.

Caleb was Kennizite, one of the clans of Esau. He was a man of faith and valor. He became a leader of the tribe of Judah. Because of his faithful service, he was granted the city and environs of Hebron as an inheritance. (Joshua 14)

His younger brother Othniel was also granted an inheritance in the territory of Judah. Othniel became Israel's first judge. (Judg. 3: 7ff)

Rahab, the harlot of Jericho, married into the tribe of Judah. She gave birth to Boaz. Boaz married the Moabite widow Ruth. Ruth and Boaz were ancestors of both King David and Jesus. (Matt. 1)

Jael was a Kenite. The Kenites were a tribe of Midianites descended from Abraham's third wife Keturah. They lived in the land in tents as semi-nomads, much as did Abraham, Isaac, and Jacob. Jael is the hero in the story of Deborah (Judg. 4)

The Kenites were still living in the land 400 years later in the time of Jeremiah. They were still *"keeping the way of the Lord and doing what is right and just."*

These were all children of Promise, not by biological descent, but by faith. They all shared the Land of Promise.

Sharing the Land: I have heard some Christian Zionists say: "God gave the land to the Jewish people, period!" They dismiss the Arabs as mere squatters on Israel's land. The Arabs should go somewhere else and leave the land to the Jewish people.

The Bible and history tell a very different story. **Israel was never in its long history the sole occupant of the Land of Promise.**

Abraham himself shared the land with Hittites, Hurrians, and Amorites. (Gen. 23)

The Israelites coming from Egypt did not succeed in purging the land of its Canaanite population. In Joshua we read:

> They did not dislodge the Canaanites that lived in Gezer; to this day the Canaanites live among the people of Ephraim but are required to do forced labor. (Joshua 16:10.)

Caleb, Othniel, Rahab, and Jael are only a few examples of the many non-Israelites who have shared the land with Jacob's children. They were descendants of Abraham, but not of Isaac or Jacob. They qualified, however, because they *"kept the way of the Lord by doing what is right and just."* Their stories are told in the book of Judges.

The Kingdom of Israel reached its greatest extent in the time of David and Solomon. These two great kings subdued their non-Israelite neighbors. But they did not destroy or expel them. The Philistines continued to occupy the coastal plain. Some even served as David's palace guard.

The prophet Ezekiel knew that Jews returning from Babylonian exile would be sharing the land with non-Jews. He made provisions for these foreigners who had *"settled among you and who have children."* They were to share the land with their Jewish neighbors, as we discussed back in chapter 14.

In Jesus' time, the Galilee was called "Galilee of the Nations" because of its large Gentile population.

The Jewish people of today will have to share the land with others, as they have throughout history. The question is: Will Israelis and Palestinians share the land as friends, or as enemies?

THE ULTIMATE OWNER

The Jewish people have a biblical claim to the Land of Promise. But this claim is neither absolute nor exclusive. God is the ultimate owner of the land. He told the Israelites: *"The land is mine, and you are but aliens and my tenants."* (Lev. 25:23)

In fact, this applies to all lands everywhere: *"The earth is the Lord's and everything in it; the world, and all who live in it."* (Ps. 24:1)

God has never surrendered his title to the land. He is the landlord of planet earth; we are his tenants. As the landlord, God has set conditions for those who would *"live long upon the land the Lord your God is giving you."* (Exo. 20: 12)

Jeremiah told his fellow Jews:

> *"If you really change your ways and your actions and deal with each other justly, if you* **do not oppress the alien,** *the fatherless or the widow and do not shed innocent blood in this place...then I will let you live in this place, the land I gave your forefathers forever and ever.* (Jer. 7: 5-7)

Jewish settlers are not doing what is *"right and just"* when they deprive Palestinians of ther lands and homes. Palestinians are not doing what is *"right and just"* when they send suicide bombers or rockets into Israeli cities. Neither are *"keeping the way of the Lord,"* as is required of Abraham's children.

The Landlord declares:

> *You and the alien shall be the same before the Lord: The same laws and regulations will apply to you and to the alien living among you.* (Num. 15:16)

> *Do not mistreat the alien or oppress him, for you were aliens in Egypt.* (Deut. 19:14).

Israelis and Palestinians must answer for their actions to the ultimate landlord.

Love vs lust for the land: To love the land is one thing. To **lust** for the land is another. There is a difference.

The prophets of Judah had a word for those who **lusted** for the land:

> *Woe to you who join house to house and field to field till no space is left and you live alone in the land.* (Isa. 5:8)

> *They covet fields, and seize them, and houses, and take them. They defraud a man of his home, a fellow man of his inheritance.* (Mic. 2:2)

What Isaiah and Micah denounced is happening today, as Jewish settlements continue to expand in the occupied territories, *"until no space is left"* for the Palesinians. That is a **lust** for the land; not love.

LOVE MY LAND; LOVE MY PEOPLE

God requires that those who love the land must also love the people of the land. The Torah commands all who dwell therein to *"love your neighbor as yourself"* and to *"love the alien as yourself."* (Lev. 19:18,34)

The hardest words in the Bible: Jesus extends this command to *"Love your **enemies**."*

These are very difficult words. It is very hard, perhaps impossible to love those you believe are trying to kill you. Or to love those who have deprived you of your homeland.

Both Israelis and Palestinians see their very existence

under dire threat. Both see the other as the unwanted "alien" in the land. There are plenty of scars and still bleeding wounds in both sides from decades of bitter conflict.

Healing these wounds will require a settlement that stops the bloodshed, allows Israelis to feel secure, and allows Palestinians to live as a free people in the land.

Even then, it will take time to heal all these wounds. But God is "ever merciful and compassionate to all." His grace is sufficient for all our needs.

Grace and Peace: Isaiah had a vision of a time when these wounds would finally heal. Commerce would flow throughout a peaceful Middle East. Israel would be a part of this commerce.

My faith tells me God has a redemptive purpose for both Israelis and Palestinians. There is room enough in God's heart for both peoples of this troubled land.

I believe that it is God's intention for Israelis and Palestinians to share the land of promise in peace. Biblical prophecy points to this possibility, as I discuss in my previous book, *The Days of the Prophets—What We Can Learn from Biblical Prophecy.* (Teeter 2009)

Biblical prophecy tells us our options and where they lead, but it does not dictate our choices. Israel and Palestine have some hard choices to make. There is a path of peace for Israel and Palestine. It is a rocky path, with many pitfalls, and over some hard ground. But peace is attainable, if the two sides can reconcile themselves to sharing the Land of Promise.

I hope and pray that Israelis and Palestinians will make those hard choices that lead to peace.

Bibliography

Ali, Maulana Muhammad. *The Holy Quran with English Translations and Commentary.* Dublin, Ohio: Ahadiyya Anjuman Isha'at Islam Lahore Inc,. 1963.

Arberry, A.J. *The Koran Interpreted.* New York: Touchstone, 1955.

Colbi, Saul P. *Christianity in the Holy Land.* Tel-Aviv: Am Hassefer Publishers Ltd., 1969.

Conn, Harvey. "The Muslim Convert and His Culture." *The Gospel and Islam.* Monrovia: MARC, 1978. 97-113.

Fraser, David A. "An Ingel Scale for Muslim Work." *The Gospel and Islam.* Monrovia: MARC, 1978. 164-181.

Grossman, Natun, Transl. by Steven Cox. *The Jewish Paradox.* Grosset & Dunlap, 1978

Khalidi, Haazam Muhammad, Dr. Jerusalem: Unpublished lecture notes, 1979.

Khalidi, Tarif. *The Muslim Jesus.* Cambridge: Harvard University Press, 2001.

—. *The Quran - A New Translation.* London: Penguin Books, 2008.

Khan, Zafrulla. *The Quran. Surrey:* Biddles Ltd, 1970.

Kraft, Charles. "Dynamic Equivalent Churches in Muslim Society. *The Gospel and Islam: A 1978 Compendium.* Monrovia: MARC, 1978 114

McCurry, Don. "A Time for New Beginnings." *The Gospel and Islam.* Monrovia: MARC, 1978. 11-21.

McCurry, Don M., Editor. *The Gospel and Islam: A 1978 Compendium.* Monrovia: MARC, 1978.

Meir, Golda. From a speech to the Israeli Knesset, 1969.

Parshall, Phil. *Bridges To Islam.* Grand Rapids: Baker Book House, 1983.

—. New Paths In Muslim Evangelism. Grand Rapids: Baker, 1980.

Richardson, Don. *Eternity In Their Hearts.* Ventura`: Regal, 1981.

Teeter, David. T*he Days of the Prophets – What We Can Learn From Biblical Prophecy.* Denver: Outskirts Press, 2009

LaVergne, TN USA
24 August 2009

155750LV00001B/29/P